"There are many good theologians in the church today, and many teachers who love children. But few are a combination of both like Marty Machowski. I am delighted to commend this engaging resource to help all of us know and worship the God of the Bible!"

JUSTIN TAYLOR, Managing editor, *ESV Study Bible*; coauthor, *The Final Days of Jesus*

"*The Ology* is a beautifully illustrated book. That in itself will hold the attention of children. But the words carefully unfold the teaching of Scripture in a way that doesn't talk down to children but talks to them, lifting up their understanding of the triune God as Creator and Redeemer. Marty Machowski has given the church a valuable resource for parents and others wanting to disciple the young."

RICHARD B. GAFFIN, JR., Professor of Biblical and Systematic Theology, Emeritus Westminster Theological Seminary

"This marvelous book works on every level: It is thoroughly biblical, doctrinally sound, gospel-centered, well written, and exquisitely illustrated. I intend to buy this book for my grandchildren and read it together with them over and over and over again. I can't give *The Ology* a higher endorsement than that!"

GREGG R. ALLISON, Professor of Christian Theology, The Southern Baptist Theological Seminary; secretary of the Evangelical Theological Society; pastor and author

"This well-illustrated book clearly and logically introduces theology for children."

ANDY NASELLI, Assistant Professor of New Testament and Biblical Theology at Bethlehem College & Seminary in Minneapolis

"*The Ology* is a great answer to the dilemma of how parents can introduce their children to biblical theology. Marty Machowski brings solid reformed theological truth into a most attractive and understandable format. Parents everywhere will rejoice to see their children 'get it' as they work through *The Ology* together."

GERRY BRESHEARS, Professor of Theology, Western Seminary, Portland

"*The Ology* uses story and art to make scriptural truth understandable and real to all of God's children, regardless of age. I eagerly look forward to reading *The Ology* with my grandson!"

R. J. GORE JR., Professor of Systematic Theology and Acting Dean Erskine Theological Seminary, Due West, SC

"*The Ology* is biblically saturated, theologically rich, clearly written, and helpfully illustrated. May the Spirit use this book to establish the next generation on the rock of God's Word and produce disciples who follow Jesus for a lifetime!"

MATTHEW S. HARMON, Professor of New Testament Studies, Grace Theological Seminary

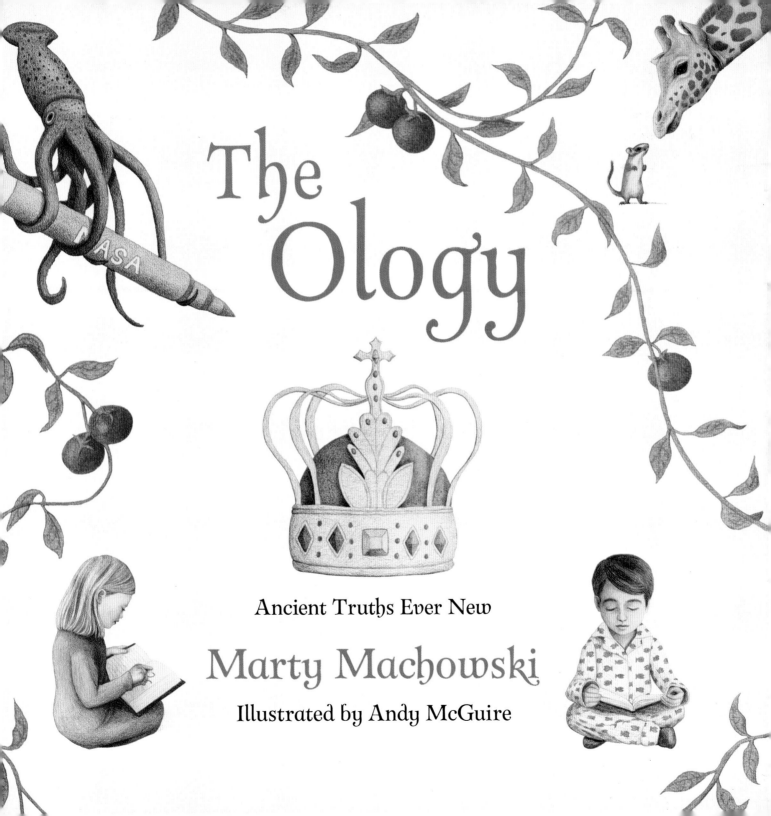

The Ology

Ancient Truths Ever New

Marty Machowski

Illustrated by Andy McGuire

New
Growth
Press

New Growth Press, Greensboro, NC 27404
Text Copyright © 2015 by Marty Machowski.
Illustration Copyright © 2015 by Andy McGuire

Cover art: Andy McGuire
Interior art: Andy McGuire
Cover/Interior Design and Typesetting: Faceout Books, faceoutstudio.com

ISBN: 978-1-942572-28-2 (Print)
ISBN: 978-1-942572-57-2 (eBook)

Library of Congress Cataloging-in-Publication Data

Machowski, Martin, 1963-
The ology : ancient truths ever new / Marty Machowski.
    pages cm
ISBN 978-1-942572-28-2
1. Theology, Doctrinal. 2. Christian education of children. I. Title.
BT75.3.M275 2015
248.8'45--dc23
                        2015004165

Printed in China

23 22 21 20 19 18 17 16   3 4 5 6 7

Contents

Acknowledgments

I would like to share my appreciation for the team of folks who made this book possible. Barbara Juliani and Nancy Winter helped me communicate complex theological concepts in ways that children can better understand. My wife, Lois, read every page, offering her helpful suggestions. The administrative staff at Covenant Fellowship offered their critique and enthusiastic support as I read them each page as it was completed.

I'd also like to thank Wayne Grudem for his books, *Systematic Theology* and *Bible Doctrine*, which served as my foundational resources. It was in reading *Bible Doctrine* with my teenage children that my desire grew to make these deep theological truths accessible to a younger generation.

Andy McGuire did a spectacular job creating wonderful illustrations, which make this book fun for kids to read. Thank you, Andy, for your creativity, skill, and diligence in illustrating this project.

Finally, I would like to acknowledge the many pastors whose sermons have soaked into my soul and shaped my life over the thirty years of my Christian walk. Know that your labors in study will now bear fruit in the lives of multiple children who pick up and read this book.

Parent Guide

As a parent picking up this book, you may be wondering if your children are too young to study theology. Theology is simply the study of God. Whether you realize it or not, our children learn about God every day. We teach them about God's power and beauty when we marvel at a rainbow or the power of the ocean waves. We teach them about God when we explain right from wrong, or how to pray before bedtime, and the importance of forgiving a friend. This book lays out theology in a simple and clear way that presents deep, important truths about God in an easy-to-understand format for you and your children.

The Ology is a multilayered educational resource for grade school children. While the illustrations are geared to the younger grades, Bible references provide another layer of learning to extend the use of this book for upper elementary students. Each chapter looks at a different topic. So, although they are short, it might be good to stick with one chapter a day. Then take some time throughout your day to discuss the different things your children are learning about God with them.

Early elementary students (ages 6–9). Parents of first graders can read the book straight through from cover to cover the first time, then come back to individual topics and ask their children about the illustrations, helping the children to connect the artwork with the truths the pages present. The more abstract theological truths are presented with easier to understand analogies, so that the youngest children can begin to learn the concepts presented through them.

The Ology is a perfect book to challenge early readers and expand their theological vocabulary. Of course they will need a little help. So we've defined some important theological words in a glossary at the back of the book and provided kid-friendly definitions to these words. This should help children understand these concepts so they become a part of their vocabulary.

The early elementary age is also the time to point out the Bible references and use them to talk about how the theological truths contained in *The Ology* are all found in the Bible.

Ask children if they know if a particular reference is from the Old or New Testament, and see if they can learn the correct genre of literature—narrative (historical stories), poetry (Psalms), wisdom (Proverbs, Job, Ecclesiastes), law (Exodus, Leviticus, Numbers, Deuteronomy), prophetic (Isaiah to Malachi), gospel (Matthew to John), letters (Romans to Jude), apocalyptic (Revelation).

Also, use the discussion questions in the "Think Theology Talk Theology" section for this age group. While children in the younger elementary grades won't be able to answer those questions in writing, you can use them in conversation as you read through each section.

As you go through the book, ask the children to repeat the Scriptures and see if they can connect them to the larger truth presented.

Upper elementary students (ages 10–12). *The Ology* can be used to teach upper elementary students systematic theology. (You could even use *The Ology* as the basis for a Bible curriculum.)

Once students have read through the book to get a big picture view of the theological landscape, have them read it through again, section by section, looking up the Scripture references.

Give them a journal in which they can list Scriptures and explain how they connect to the larger truth presented in each section.

In addition to looking up the Scriptures, have children write out answers to the discussion questions included in the "Think Theology Talk Theology" section. If you are using *The Ology* as a Bible curriculum, their answers can be used as homework.

Scripture memory. Children of all ages can memorize Scripture. *The Ology* can be used as a resource for Scripture memory by having your children memorize the verses written out on the pages. Choose one from each section to memorize along with the written work that they do.

Teens and adults. *The Ology* is a children's book, however, it can be helpful to provide the framework for a solid biblical worldview for teens and young adults as well. Assign it to high school students as a children's book (they will not be fooled) and have them write a paper on the worldview presented within its pages and whether they agree or disagree and why.

If you are looking for the next step beyond *The Ology,* consider *Big Truths for Young Hearts* by Bruce Ware and *Bible Doctrine* by Wayne Grudem.

There is also a companion album to *The Ology* by Sovereign Grace Music that celebrates these wonderful theological truths through worship music that the whole family can enjoy. You can purchase it at http://sovereigngracemusic.org.

Where it all began...

Exploring the centuries-old church in their neighborhood was proving to be an adventure that Carla and Timothy would not soon forget. They had come upon an unlocked cellar door and had ventured down the stone stairway into the musty dimness below.

"Look!" Carla exclaimed as she lifted the corner of a thick rug. "A hidden door."

"I wonder where it leads," Timothy said. "Does it open?"

The children pulled back the rug and lifted the door. Timothy pointed his flashlight into the darkness revealing a stairway to a room beneath the church cellar.

Cautiously they crept down the stairs into a small, musty storage room. In the dim light they could see a low table covered with a colorful cloth. Perched on the table was an old candelabrum.

Carla stared and then exclaimed, "Look! There's something next to the candlestick!"

The children approached the table to get a better look at what lay on it. It was a package, wrapped in brown paper and tied with a string. Tucked beneath the string was a folded piece of yellowed parchment. Written on it was the instruction: Open and Read.

The two children grabbed the package, climbed back up the stairs, and sat with it in a pool of light that streamed in from one of the high basement windows. Once settled, Carla slipped the note out from under the string, opened it with care, and began to read.

To the finder of the parcel:

You hold in your hands the last known copy of a rare children's book with a long history. Its story begins with the early church pastors. They were th[e] [wh]o understand the message of [wh]o first taught us how [t]o understand the [B]ible. Later came those [wh]o studied God and the [B]ible so they could help others [B]ible so they could help others understand who God is and

To the finder of the parcel:

You hold in your hands the last known copy of a rare children's book with a long history. Its story begins with the early church pastors. They were the ones who first taught us how to understand the message of the Bible. Later came those who studied God and the Bible so they could help others understand who God is and how to follow him. Just a few of them were Thomas Aquinas, Martin Luther, and John Calvin. Because they studied God, people started calling them theologians. Theology means the study of God.

Those who were helped by their writings wanted to pass these truths on to their children. And so they wrote a book for children, entitled The Ology, *so that they too might understand deep truths about God, drawn from the Bible.* The Ology *teaches us what the Bible says about God, people, sin, and God's plan of salvation through Jesus. When children read it, they loved it! It helped them to understand who God is, how much he loves them, and how to follow him.*

But sadly, after many years, The Ology *was forgotten. Parents and children began to think the truths of* The Ology *were old-fashioned and out of date. One by one these books vanished. The book you now hold may be the very last copy of* The Ology *in existence.*

I placed this wrapped copy in the storage cellar, and I offer it as a gift to the finder. Open it and read it carefully. My prayer is that it will help you to know God and know yourself. But most of all I pray that you will know how much God loves you. His love never fails!

Yours truly,

Jonathan E.

The children sat unmoving, not sure if they should unwrap the book. Then Carla said, "What do you think; should we open it?"

"I say yes," Timothy answered.

Carefully they untied the string and removed the paper wrapping. The book's ornate leather cover had a two-word title: *The Ology*. In small type at the bottom of the cover were four more words: "Ancient Truths Ever New." Opening the book to the beginning they saw words, but the ornate type was hard to read. They stared at the page trying to decipher the text, but then suddenly, in unison, the children blinked in astonishment. The page was changing before their eyes. The words became easy to read and colorful images brightened the page. The ancient pages became like the pages of a brand new book!

The Ology
of God

Deuteronomy 33:27

Genesis 21:33

1 Timothy 1:17

Psalm 100:5

Psalm 102:25–27

1. God Always Was and Always Will Be

Oak trees sprout from acorns and toads begin as tadpoles, but God never had a beginning. When you look at photos of yourself that were taken years ago, you can see how much you've grown and changed. But there was never a time when God was smaller or younger. God is the same today as he was yesterday, and God will be the same tomorrow.

The day ends when the clock strikes twelve. The race ends at the finish line. But God will never end. God has always lived, and he will always live. That means that God is *eternal*. No matter how far you think back into the distant past, God has always lived. No matter how far you think ahead into the distant future, God will always be there.

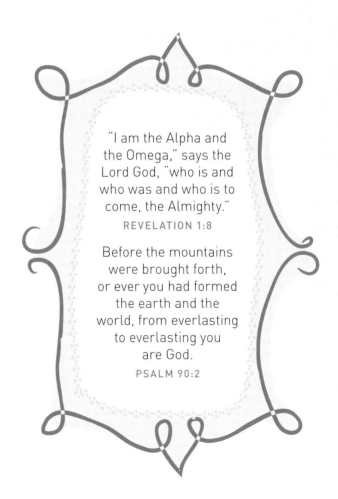

"I am the Alpha and the Omega," says the Lord God, "who is and who was and who is to come, the Almighty."
REVELATION 1:8

Before the mountains were brought forth, or ever you had formed the earth and the world, from everlasting to everlasting you are God.
PSALM 90:2

Names are special. That is why when you write your name, you start with a capital letter, like the "J" in Jack or the "S" in Sophie. That is also why we write an upper case "G" when we write about the one true God.

The names of Bible characters often tell us something about a person. Abraham means "the father of many," and he became the father of God's people. In the Bible, God himself, who can't be described by just one word or name, has many names; for example, Almighty, Bread of Life, Counselor, Deliverer, Everlasting Father, Fountain, Good Shepherd, Holy One, Immanuel, Jesus, King of Kings, Light of the World, Mighty God, Prince of Peace, Rock, Savior, Truth, Vine, Wonderful Counselor, and Lamb. God is even named the Alpha and Omega, after the first and last letters of the Greek alphabet because he is the first and the last. Each of the names the Bible uses to describe God tells us something about who he is.

For to us a child is born, to us a son is given; and the government shall be upon his shoulder, and his name shall be called Wonderful Counselor, Mighty God, Everlasting Father, Prince of Peace.

ISAIAH 9:6

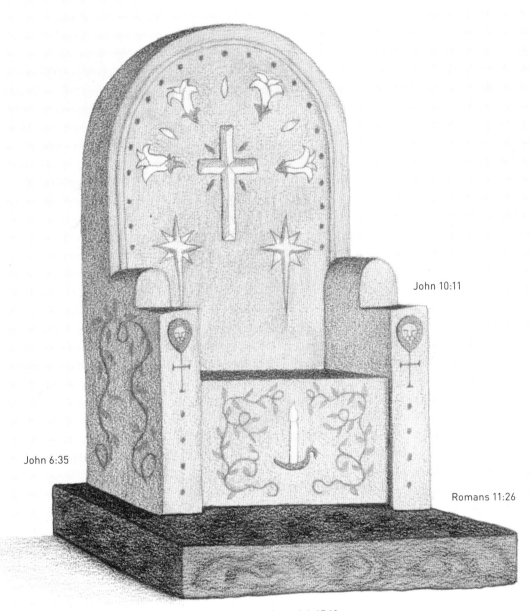

John 10:11

John 6:35

Romans 11:26

Jeremiah 17:13

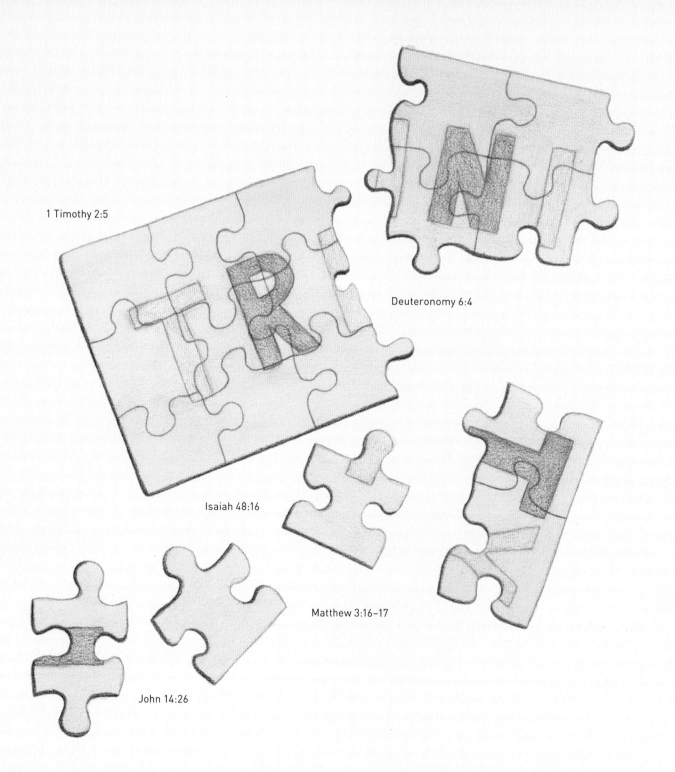

1 Timothy 2:5

Deuteronomy 6:4

Isaiah 48:16

Matthew 3:16–17

John 14:26

2. God Is Three in One

When you put together a jigsaw puzzle, you have to figure out how all the different pieces fit together to make a picture. God can be like that. The truths that the Bible tells us about God are a little bit like pieces of a puzzle. The more we learn about God, the clearer our picture of him will be, the more amazing he becomes to us, and the more we love him.

Here are a few truths about God, written in a poem. Read each line on its own and see if you can understand it, then read them all together:

The Bible teaches that our God is one,
Made up of three; Father, Spirit, and Son.
The Father and Son are one, it is true!
The Son and the Spirit, also one too.
Each one is distinct, yet fully divine,
United eternal in love for all time.
Trinity means the three persons are One;
Our one God is Father, Spirit, and Son.

God the Father, God the Son, and God the Holy Spirit are distinct persons, but they are equally God. Each person in the Trinity shines forth the glory of the others. The Father glorified the Son when at Jesus's transfiguration he told us to listen to the Son. The Son shined forth the glory of the Father by going all the way to the cross out of love for his Father and for us. The Spirit shines forth the glory of the Son as he reminds us of all that Jesus taught and makes us shine like Jesus too. Each person in the Trinity loves the others in an eternal love relationship. That's one of the reasons that the Bible tells us that God is love!

One day, we will see God face to face and enjoy the same pure love the Father, Son and Spirit share with each other.

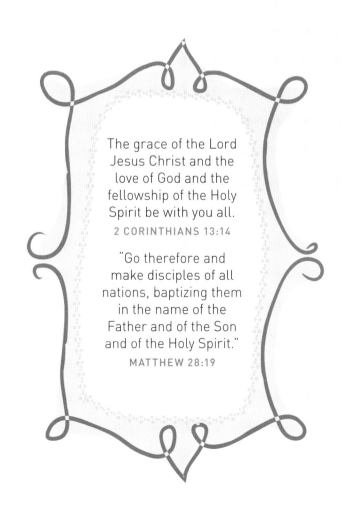

The grace of the Lord Jesus Christ and the love of God and the fellowship of the Holy Spirit be with you all.
2 CORINTHIANS 13:14

"Go therefore and make disciples of all nations, baptizing them in the name of the Father and of the Son and of the Holy Spirit."
MATTHEW 28:19

3. God Created Everything out of Nothing at All

Every created thing started the same way, with a design. A design is an idea of how to make something—a chair, a flower, or a book. You can build your design out of something. You can roll clay into a snake or fold paper into an airplane. But when God created the world, he did something no one else can do: he created everything out of nothing at all. He didn't build the universe with clay, wood, or stone, for he hadn't made them yet. He didn't start with air or water, because they had to be created too.

Did you know that you are a part of God's grand design? Before God placed a single star in the sky, he thought of you. He planned the color of your hair, how tall you would be, and the exact place where you would live. Color your thumb with a marker, press it onto paper, and notice how the lines swirl. Your fingerprint is unique to you! No one else in the whole world has your exact fingerprint. God designed it especially for you.

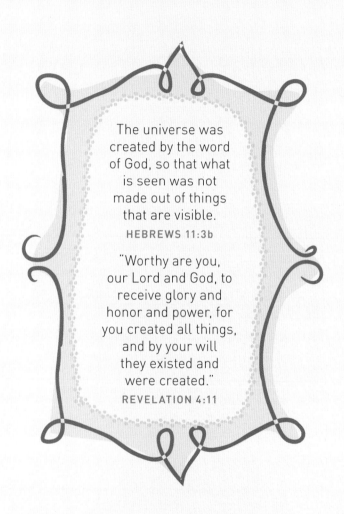

The universe was created by the word of God, so that what is seen was not made out of things that are visible.
HEBREWS 11:3b

"Worthy are you, our Lord and God, to receive glory and honor and power, for you created all things, and by your will they existed and were created."
REVELATION 4:11

Acts 4:24

Genesis 1:1

Colossians 1:16

Colossians 1:16

Romans 4:17

Psalm 139:16

Psalm 91:11–12

Psalm 148:2–5

Hebrews 13:2

Nehemiah 9:6

Isaiah 6:2–3

Revelation 4:8

Did you know that God also created wonderful creatures in the heavens? We can't see them now, but mighty angels, seraphim, and cherubim serve and worship him around his throne.

God gives his angels the job of watching over his people on earth. God also uses angels to deliver messages to people. Sometimes God allows his angels to be seen, which usually frightens folks at first, but most of the time God's angels do his work in secret.

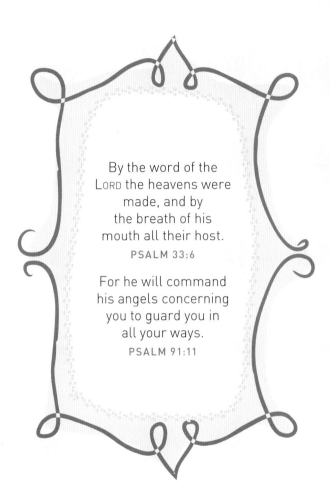

By the word of the LORD the heavens were made, and by the breath of his mouth all their host.
PSALM 33:6

For he will command his angels concerning you to guard you in all your ways.
PSALM 91:11

4. God Is All-Powerful

God is so powerful that when the time came for him to create the universe, all he used was his words. God said, "Let there be light," and there was light. How's that for powerful? With just a few words God created light, heavens, earth, sun, moon, stars, oceans, plants, fish, birds, and animals.

When God spoke, "It was so." So when God said, "Let there be light," he didn't have to wait for the light to turn on. When he said, "Let the earth bring forth living creatures," he didn't have to wait for them to be born, they appeared instantly. Imagine a forest, empty one moment and the next teeming with lions, lizards, gorillas, grasshoppers, snakes, mice, snails, butterflies, and giraffes. The Bible tells us that we can know God is real and powerful just by looking at what he created.

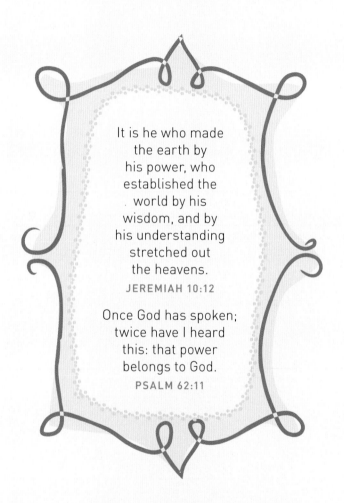

It is he who made the earth by his power, who established the world by his wisdom, and by his understanding stretched out the heavens.

JEREMIAH 10:12

Once God has spoken; twice have I heard this: that power belongs to God.

PSALM 62:11

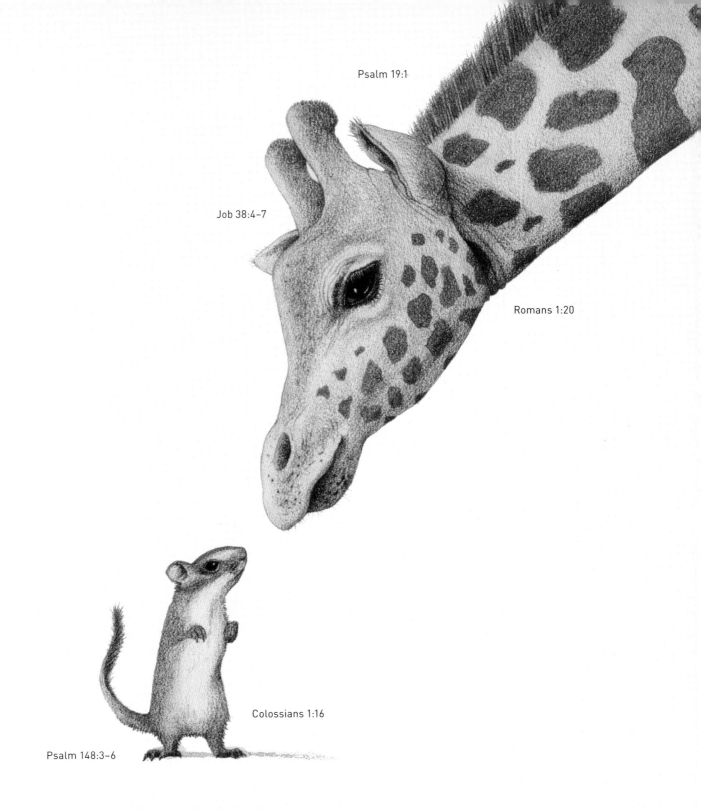

Psalm 19:1

Job 38:4–7

Romans 1:20

Colossians 1:16

Psalm 148:3–6

Acts 17:24–28

Psalm 99:3

Psalm 103:19

Isaiah 46:9–10

Job 37:5–6

5. God Is in Control

From the grain of sand tossed by the ocean waves, to the stars in the far reaches of the universe, God, like the conductor of an orchestra, is at work directing each part of his creation. Nothing moves without his command, and nothing happens outside his control. He commands every rain shower and snowfall; he tells the flower buds to bloom and the ocean waves to roll. No one, not even the angels in heaven, can stop God's work in our world.

Every minute of every day, God holds the universe together by the word of his power. God is keeping his creation steady so that everything works according to his plan. Rocks are still hard like God planned them to be, and the water still drops and drips like it was designed. While dogs come in different colors, shapes, and sizes, they have always been dogs, just as God created them. Because God is in control, and rules over all, they will never turn into cats, just like cats can't become giraffes.

He upholds the universe by the word of his power.
HEBREWS 1:3b

In him all things hold together.
COLOSSIANS 1:17b

6. God Knows All Things

There are more stars than anyone can count, but God knows them each by name. A million sparrows flit and fly, but not one can fall outside God's control. God owns the cattle on a thousand hills and sets the limits for the ocean tide. He knows your name, planned where you would live, and could tell you any morning the number of hairs on your head. He knows the exact number of days you will live and how each one of them will go.

God knows everything about everything and everything about everybody. Nothing ever surprises him and he always knows what to do. God knows what will happen tomorrow—what time you will wake up and what you will eat for breakfast. He has already planned how to use everything in your life for good—even those things we don't want to happen. How can God know all these things? Because he is God—God with a capital "G"!

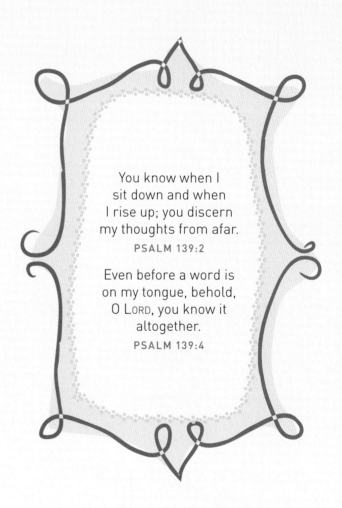

You know when I sit down and when I rise up; you discern my thoughts from afar.
PSALM 139:2

Even before a word is on my tongue, behold, O LORD, you know it altogether.
PSALM 139:4

Hebrews 4:13

1 John 3:20

Acts 17:26

PROPERTY OF GOD

Matthew 10:29–30

Psalm 147:4

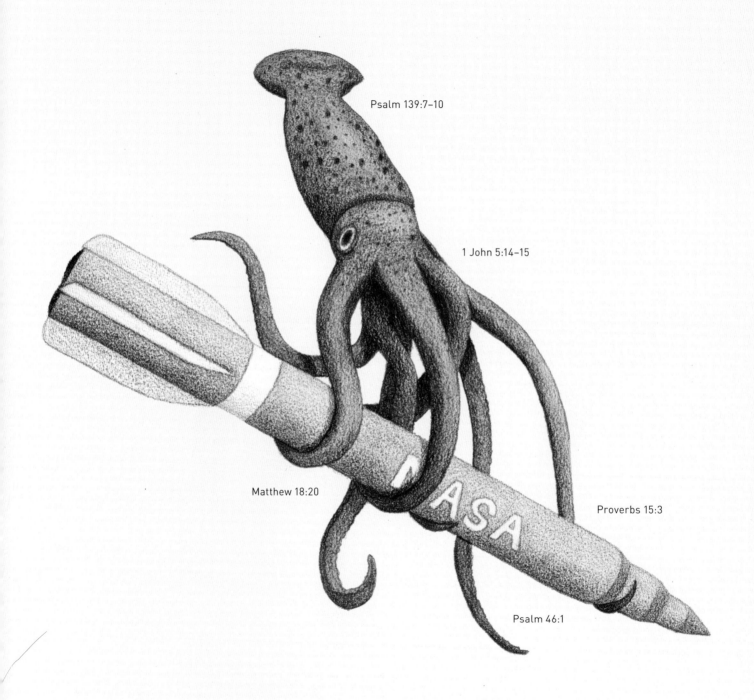

Psalm 139:7–10

1 John 5:14–15

Matthew 18:20

Proverbs 15:3

Psalm 46:1

7. God Is Everywhere

God is everywhere. That means wherever you are, you can count on God and call on him. If you climb the highest mountain, God is there. If you sink to the bottom of the ocean, God is there. If you travel to a space station, God is there. This also means there is no place you can ever hide from God.

Because God is everywhere, he knows what you are happy about and what you are sad about. He knows everything about every person, in every country, all at the same time! Any of God's children can pray to him at any time and be certain that he hears them!

If I take the wings of the morning and dwell in the uttermost parts of the sea, even there your hand shall lead me, and your right hand shall hold me.
PSALM 139:9–10

Can a man hide himself in secret places so that I cannot see him? declares the Lord. Do I not fill heaven and earth? declares the Lord.
JEREMIAH 23:24

8. God Is Perfect

When something is perfect, there is nothing bad about it. Period. A perfectly white shirt has no spots or stains. A perfect shot hits the very center of the target.

Our God is perfect in every way. If he were an archer, his arrows would hit the exact center of the target every time. God always tells the truth. God is perfectly just—that means he knows when people are wrong and he knows exactly what to do about it. God is perfectly holy and good—that means he is against everything that is wrong, bad, and evil.

The most wonderful perfection of God is his love. Baking a cake requires mixing together ingredients like flour, sugar, oil, eggs, and water. God's perfect love is like that; it is a mix of faithfulness, grace, forgiveness, kindness, generosity, sacrifice, humility, truth, patience, and hope.

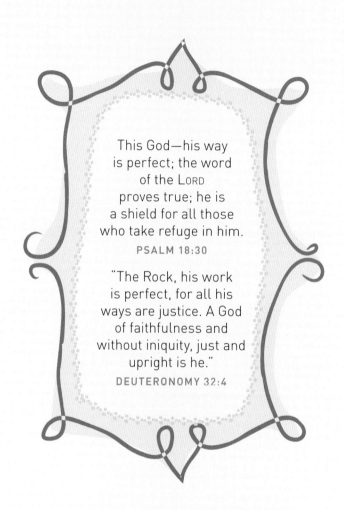

This God—his way is perfect; the word of the LORD proves true; he is a shield for all those who take refuge in him.

PSALM 18:30

"The Rock, his work is perfect, for all his ways are justice. A God of faithfulness and without iniquity, just and upright is he."

DEUTERONOMY 32:4

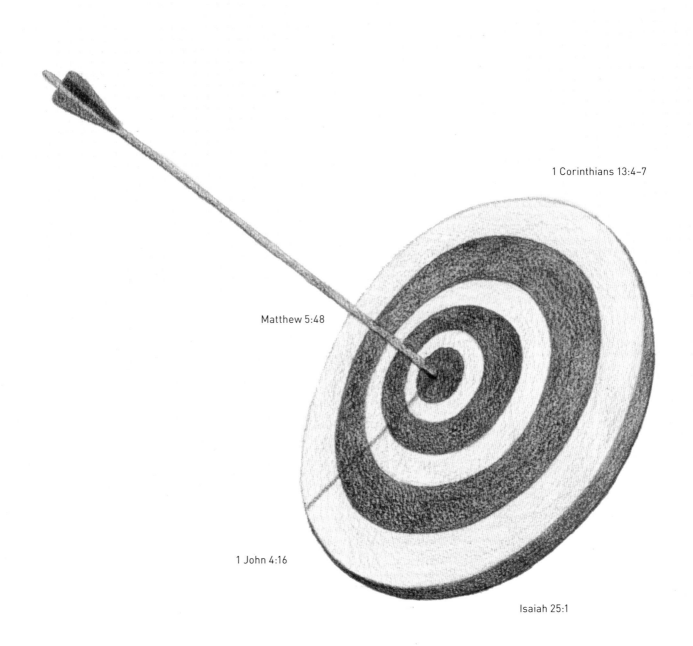

1 Corinthians 13:4–7

Matthew 5:48

1 John 4:16

Isaiah 25:1

The Ology
of People

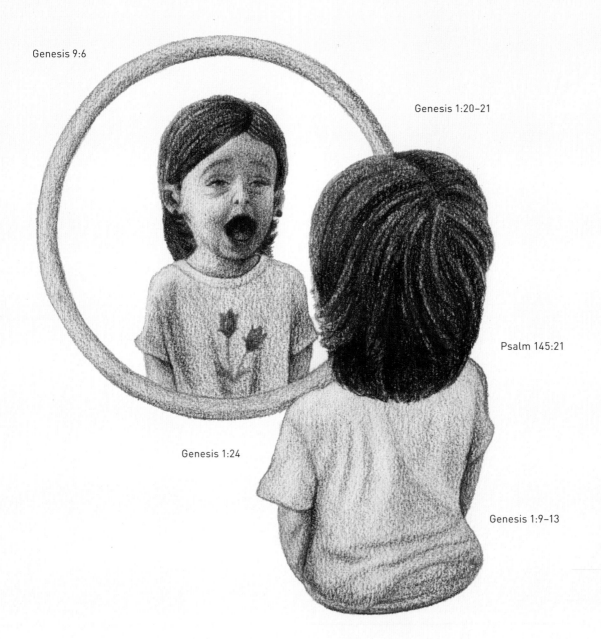

Genesis 9:6

Genesis 1:20–21

Psalm 145:21

Genesis 1:24

Genesis 1:9–13

9. God Created Man and Woman in His Image

When you look in a mirror, you see your image. If you smile, your image smiles right back. The Bible tells us that all people are created in God's image. But what does that mean? For one thing, people look very different from each other. We are girls and boys, dark-skinned and light-skinned, tall and short, blond and brunette, and so forth.

But while we have differences in the way we look, there are a lot of ways we are all the same and reflect the image of God. God can speak; we can too. Like God, we can create and invent things. But the most important way we reflect God's image is that we can love.

We can love God and one another. God is a God of relationship. For all time God has been a loving Father and Son, enjoying one another in relationship with the Holy Spirit. He made us to be like him, enjoying him and enjoying one another in friendship, marriage, and family.

Then God said, "Let us make man in our image, after our likeness."
GENESIS 1:26

When God created mankind, he made them in the likeness of God. He created them male and female and blessed them. And he named them "Mankind" when they were created.
GENESIS 5:1–2 NIV

After creating the animals by speaking, God did something very different to make the first man. God formed the first man from the dirt on the ground and then gave him a beautiful fruit-filled garden called Eden to live in. God called the first man Adam and gave him a special job, to name all the animals. Doesn't that sound like a fun job! But Adam soon became lonely, for none of the animals were, like him, made in the image of God.

Adam could do things the animals could not. He could know God and worship him. He could think up new names, and he could be in charge of the animals. Adam could understand God's words; he could sing for joy, and he could love. But he longed for someone else who could do those things too.

God, looking on, was not surprised. Knowing all along that it was not good for the man to be alone, God had a plan for a partner for him from the very beginning. Adam needed a helper.

Then the LORD God said, "It is not good that the man should be alone; I will make him a helper fit for him."

GENESIS 2:18

Genesis 5:1

Genesis 2:7–8

Genesis 2:18–20

1 Corinthians 15:49

1 Corinthians 11:3

Genesis 2:20–23

Matthew 19:5

Ephesians 5:31

10. The First Husband and Wife

God caused Adam to fall asleep and took a rib from his side and created a partner for him, a woman, also made in the image of God. She was his perfect match, for, like Adam, she could know God, worship him, and she too could love. God presented her to Adam who welcomed her with joy and gave her the name "Woman" for she was taken out of man. (Later, Adam named her Eve, which means the mother of all the living.)

Together they became the first husband and wife. Ever since then, God has commanded that when it is time to marry, a man shall "leave his father and his mother and hold fast to his wife, and they shall become one flesh."

Adam and Eve were perfectly happy. Have you ever been so happy you couldn't stop smiling? I think that is what it was like for them. They were happy with each other and they were especially happy because God was with them. They had never experienced anything sad or scary.

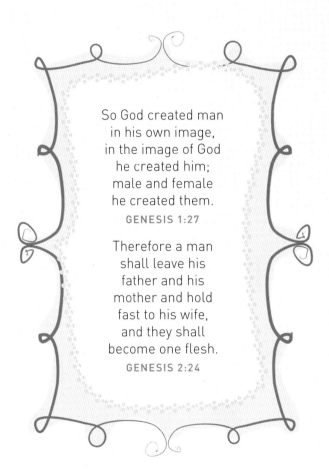

So God created man in his own image, in the image of God he created him; male and female he created them.
GENESIS 1:27

Therefore a man shall leave his father and his mother and hold fast to his wife, and they shall become one flesh.
GENESIS 2:24

11. God Walked with Adam and Eve in the Garden

Heaven is where God lives, where you can see him face-to-face. Eden was like that for Adam and Eve. They walked together, enjoying the beautiful garden filled with fruit trees. They talked about the job God had given them—to be in charge of the new world and to fill it with children and grandchildren. Everything about their life was perfect. They never got sick. There was no fighting. They were never sad or lonely. There was no death. Best of all, God also would walk and talk with them in the garden.

In the middle of the garden were two special trees: the tree of life, and the tree of the knowledge of good and evil. Adam and Eve could eat as much as they liked from the tree of life. But this was not the case for the tree of the knowledge of good and evil. God told them they could not eat the fruit of this tree; and if they did, they would die. That was a terrible thought, but there were plenty of other trees that had juicy, delicious fruit. Sadly, everything didn't stay perfect in the garden for long. Something terrible happened—sin.

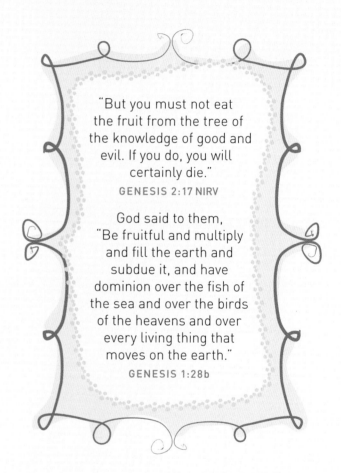

"But you must not eat the fruit from the tree of the knowledge of good and evil. If you do, you will certainly die."
GENESIS 2:17 NIRV

God said to them, "Be fruitful and multiply and fill the earth and subdue it, and have dominion over the fish of the sea and over the birds of the heavens and over every living thing that moves on the earth."
GENESIS 1:28b

Genesis 3:22

Psalm 16:11

Genesis 2:15–16

Genesis 1:29–31

The Ology
of Sin

Psalm 1:5–6

Isaiah 53:6

1 John 3:4

12. Sin

To understand sin, you have to remember that God made us to love him above anything else—above family, friends, the things we like to do, and the things we have (or want to get!). Sin is making anything in our lives more important than God. When we do that, we don't love and worship God as we were made to do. The Bible calls this going our own way. Sin starts on the inside—with what we want more than God. Did you know that the smallest sin ruins our lives just like the smallest black stain ruins a perfectly white dress? What's worse, our small sins never stay small. Any sin, if left alone, will grow. Like mold on a damp wall, it spreads and contaminates everything.

Imagine you're outside on a hot summer day and are just about to reach for a glass of ice cold, pure, crystal clear, water. Then something terrible happens: the droppings of a bird splash into your water. If that happened, what would you do? For one thing, you wouldn't drink the water. Sin is like that; even one little bit spoils everything. Since God is perfectly pure and holy, he must judge and punish any sin.

So whoever knows the right thing to do and fails to do it, for him it is sin.
JAMES 4:17

"And you shall love the Lord your God with all your heart and with all your soul and with all your mind and with all your strength."
MARK 12:30

Where did sin start? The Bible tells us that it started in heaven! How could that be? Well, here's how it happened: God created angels, beautiful, powerful creatures to serve him. The most beautiful and amazing of them all was the guardian angel God placed on the holy mountain of God. Sadly, this guardian angel became proud, turned against God, and persuaded other angels to join him in trying to take over the world from God. Wasn't it silly that they thought they could fight God?

Well of course they couldn't win a fight against God. So with lightning speed, the Bible tells us, God threw the rebel angels out of heaven, and never let them return.

Since that day the rebel angel has been called Satan, the devil. The Bible also calls Satan the father of lies and tells us that he is like a prowling lion who comes to steal, kill, and destroy. Satan tries to get us to be like him and fight against God. Since he is miserable, he wants everyone else to be miserable too! He tricked Adam and Eve into disobeying God and he is still trying to trick us today.

God did not spare angels when they sinned, but cast them into hell and committed them to chains of gloomy darkness.
2 PETER 2:4

Be sober-minded; be watchful. Your adversary the devil prowls around like a roaring lion, seeking someone to devour.
1 PETER 5:8

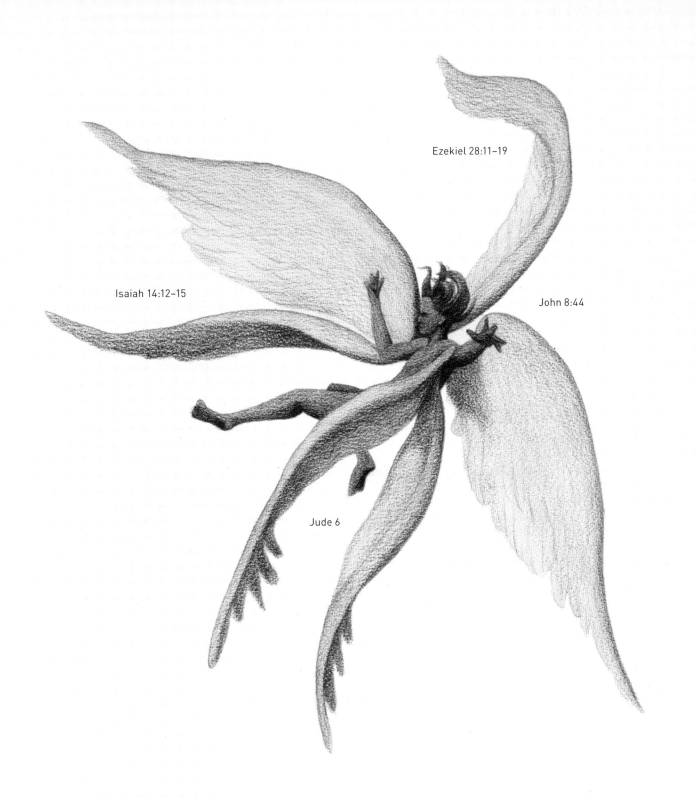

Ezekiel 28:11–19

Isaiah 14:12–15

John 8:44

Jude 6

2 Corinthians 11:3

John 8:44

James 4:7

1 John 3:8

13. Satan's First Temptation

It didn't take long for Satan to tell his lies about God to Adam and Eve. He knew God had told them not to eat from the tree of the knowledge of good and evil. Entering a serpent, an animal the Bible calls the trickiest beast of all, he headed for the forbidden tree. When Adam and Eve were nearby, the serpent called out to Eve. He tempted her by twisting God's words, trying to make her think that God was selfish and didn't want Adam and Eve to be like him. He told her that if she ate the fruit, she could become like God, knowing good and evil. Like most of Satan's temptations, his words contained a little bit of truth: Adam and Eve would know evil if they ate the fruit. But also, like all of Satan's temptations, it was a big lie.

Eve had no idea what evil or bad things were. All she knew was that it was part of the name of the forbidden tree. Satan knew that as long as she and Adam obeyed God's command they would never know evil. But he also knew that with just one taste of the fruit of the forbidden tree, all of that would change. For then the woman wouldn't just know evil, she would become evil—an enemy of God.

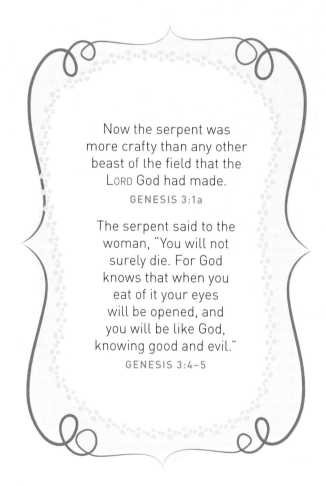

Now the serpent was more crafty than any other beast of the field that the Lord God had made.
GENESIS 3:1a

The serpent said to the woman, "You will not surely die. For God knows that when you eat of it your eyes will be opened, and you will be like God, knowing good and evil."
GENESIS 3:4–5

While the serpent watched from his perch in the tree, the woman thought about his words: "your eyes will be opened," "you can be like God." She didn't run away, which is exactly what she should have done. Nor did she call out to God for help. Instead, she decided to trust her own ideas—to decide for herself whether or not the fruit was good. That might have seemed a good idea at the time, but it was the worst idea ever. Why? Because she decided to rely on what she thought instead of believing God's words.

The fruit looked tasty to her, and the longer she looked at it the better it looked. Has that ever happened to you? The more you think about something that you know you shouldn't do, the more you want to do it. The serpent waited patiently, as the woman slowly reached her hand to touch the fruit. When nothing happened, she tightened her grip and pulled it toward her. The stem snapped, and the leaves of the branch fluttered back into place. Slowly she put the fruit to her lips and, disobeying the Lord's command, took a bite. Adam, standing nearby, said nothing.

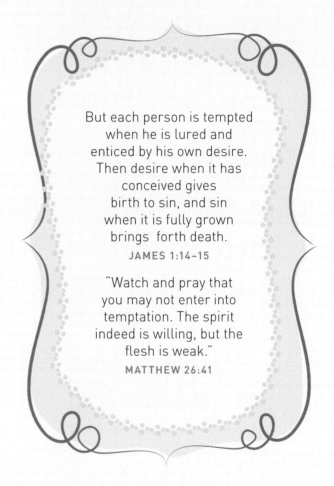

But each person is tempted when he is lured and enticed by his own desire. Then desire when it has conceived gives birth to sin, and sin when it is fully grown brings forth death.
JAMES 1:14–15

"Watch and pray that you may not enter into temptation. The spirit indeed is willing, but the flesh is weak."
MATTHEW 26:41

1 Timothy 6:9

Matthew 6:9–13

James 1:13

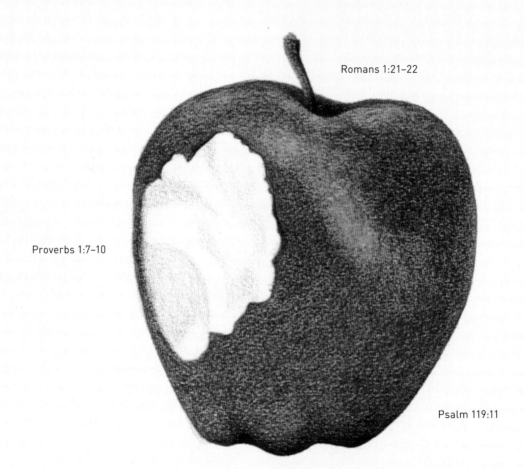

Romans 1:21–22

Proverbs 1:7–10

Psalm 119:11

Psalm 51:3–5

14. Sin Entered the World Through Adam

Eve took a bite and handed the forbidden fruit to Adam. The serpent watched as Adam took the already half-eaten fruit. Adam, by God's command, was ruler over all the earth. He was the first man and so stood for all who would come after. If Adam rebelled against God and ate the fruit, his disobedience would change the world forever. The peace, perfection, and happiness of the garden would be destroyed. His disobedience to God and the trouble that resulted would pass on to every generation to follow for they would be sinful from birth.

Adam joined his wife and bit into the fruit. For a moment they enjoyed their sin. Then, as Satan promised, Adam and Eve, who had known only good, understood evil for the first time. For the first time they noticed they were naked and felt ashamed. And for the first time they wanted to hide from God. They sewed fig leaves together to make simple clothes and hid from God.

Did you ever notice that when you do something wrong you want to hide it? That's what Adam and Eve passed on to us. We think that sinning will make us happy, but in the end we feel only guilty and ashamed. Adam and Eve wanted to be like God, but sadly, like Satan before them, they became evil, enemies of God.

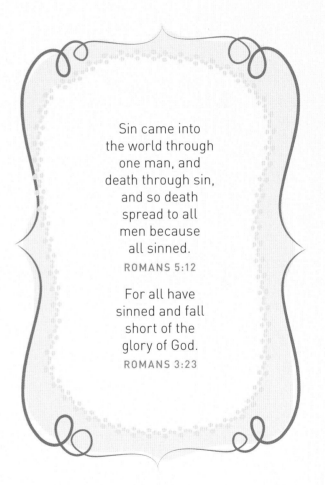

Sin came into the world through one man, and death through sin, and so death spread to all men because all sinned.
ROMANS 5:12

For all have sinned and fall short of the glory of God.
ROMANS 3:23

Ever since the day Adam ate the forbidden fruit, his sin has been passed down to every human. The Bible tells us that even newborn babies have Adam's sin passed down to them. Just like you inherited your parents' eye color, or nose, or height, you also inherited Adam's desire to go his own way instead of God's way. Adam's sin keeps getting passed down from parents to their children.

Have you noticed that no one had to teach you how to disobey or try to get your own way? Have you ever watched how little children plug their ears when they refuse to listen to their parents or get angry when they don't get what they want? They fight over toys and get mad when they don't get the one they want. Even when their parents try to protect them from being hurt—from running into the street or touching a hot stove— little children scream and yell in protest.

No one has to teach us how to tell a lie or lose control when we are angry. That is because sin comes naturally to sinners. The Bible makes it clear that ever since Adam sinned, sin became a part of who we are.

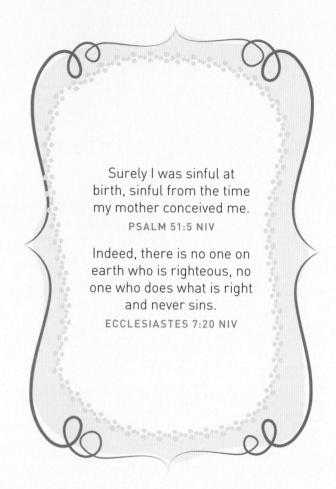

Surely I was sinful at birth, sinful from the time my mother conceived me.
PSALM 51:5 NIV

Indeed, there is no one on earth who is righteous, no one who does what is right and never sins.
ECCLESIASTES 7:20 NIV

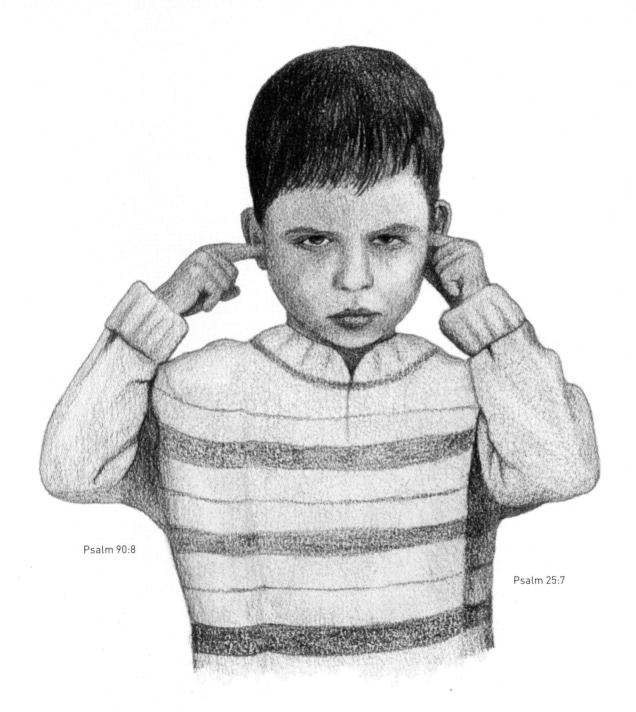

Psalm 90:8

Psalm 25:7

Galatians 5:19–21

Galatians 6:8

15. Sin Separates Us from God and from Each Other

Before their fall into sin, Adam and Eve were happy in God's world. As they walked together in the garden, they talked about the wonderful things God had made, and how one day their children would enjoy the beautiful garden. They never thought of putting on clothes because they had never done anything wrong and didn't feel guilty about anything. But after they sinned, they were filled with shame and fear.

Then they heard a fearful sound—God was looking for them. Before eating the forbidden fruit, Adam and Eve had always been happy when God came to be with them. They loved to spend time with their heavenly Father. But now they were afraid. Eating from the tree *had* given them knowledge they never had before—now they knew fear, guilt, and shame. Instead of feeling joy when they heard God coming, they felt just like children who had been caught by their parents doing something wrong. Instead of greeting God with joy, they hid among the trees. God called out for Adam. When Adam answered, he explained that they were naked and afraid.

When God asked if he had disobeyed and eaten the forbidden fruit, Adam blamed his wife. She in turn blamed the serpent, who stood defiantly, still perched in the tree. Have you ever blamed someone when you were the one who was really wrong? You inherited that from Adam and Eve!

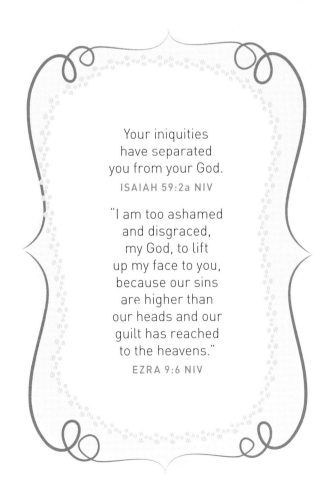

Your iniquities have separated you from your God.
ISAIAH 59:2a NIV

"I am too ashamed and disgraced, my God, to lift up my face to you, because our sins are higher than our heads and our guilt has reached to the heavens."
EZRA 9:6 NIV

Temptation and sin still work the same as they did in the garden so long ago. Satan still tempts us to believe that God doesn't want the best for us and that we don't really have to obey his rules. Satan still lies to us and tries to tell us that God doesn't love us and care for us. But now, since Adam and Eve sinned, deep inside we agree with Satan. We don't want God to tell us what to do and we don't want to listen to his Word.

Because Adam's sin was passed down to us, we all turn away from God and love the things God created more than we love God. We even get mad at God when we don't get what we want, and we try to get it for ourselves. For example, have you ever wanted something so much that you didn't care how you got it? Some people even steal things that belong to others—like a bicycle.

But doing whatever we want never makes us happy the way we think it will. Even if doing something wrong is fun in the beginning, the bad consequences of sin are always nasty in the end. Adam and Eve found out just how nasty they could be.

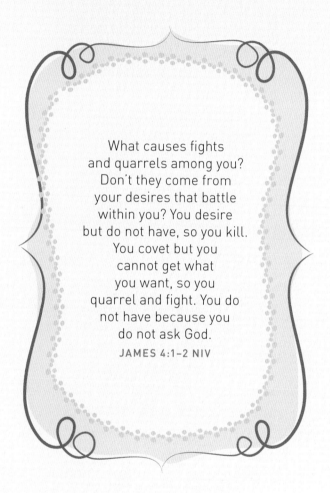

What causes fights and quarrels among you? Don't they come from your desires that battle within you? You desire but do not have, so you kill. You covet but you cannot get what you want, so you quarrel and fight. You do not have because you do not ask God.

JAMES 4:1–2 NIV

Psalm 32:5

1 Corinthians 10:13

Psalm 119:11

Ephesians 2:12

Ephesians 4:18

Genesis 3:14–15

Revelation 20:2

16. Sin Always Brings Judgment

When God found Adam and Eve hiding in the garden, they were filled with guilt and shame. This was a new and terrible experience for them. They had disobeyed God, and they were about to find out that God, not them, makes the rules for the world he created. One unchanging rule is that sin (going your own way instead of God's way) always brings judgment and death.

First, God cursed the serpent that had tempted Adam and Eve. God sentenced him to crawl on his belly. What powerful legs or beautiful wings he may have had we will never know, for as a snake he can only slither in the dust. When confronted by God, the serpent who had had plenty to say to Adam and Eve earlier, had nothing to say. But Satan wasn't done with tempting people; he would continue to deceive Adam and Eve's children and grandchildren far into the future—until the last day, when he is defeated forever.

Pride goes before destruction, and a haughty spirit before a fall.
PROVERBS 16:18 NIV

After speaking to the serpent, God turned to Eve. One consequence of her sin would be pain when she had a baby. Another was that the love and closeness with Adam would be broken. Before falling into sin, Adam and Eve agreed about everything, but now they would disagree and have a hard time getting along.

Then God spoke to Adam, correcting him for eating the forbidden fruit Eve gave to him. From that day on, God said thorns and thistles would choke Adam's fields, making his work hard.

Then as God had warned, he brought the judgment of death. Adam and Eve, who were meant to live forever, would one day die and return to the dust from which God had formed man. God did not say how much longer they would live, but they knew that death was certain. From that moment on, knowing one day they would die would remind them to trust God for each and every day.

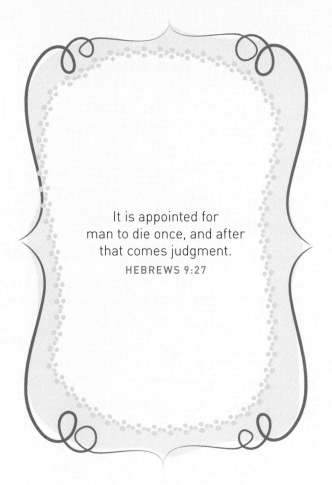

It is appointed for man to die once, and after that comes judgment.
HEBREWS 9:27

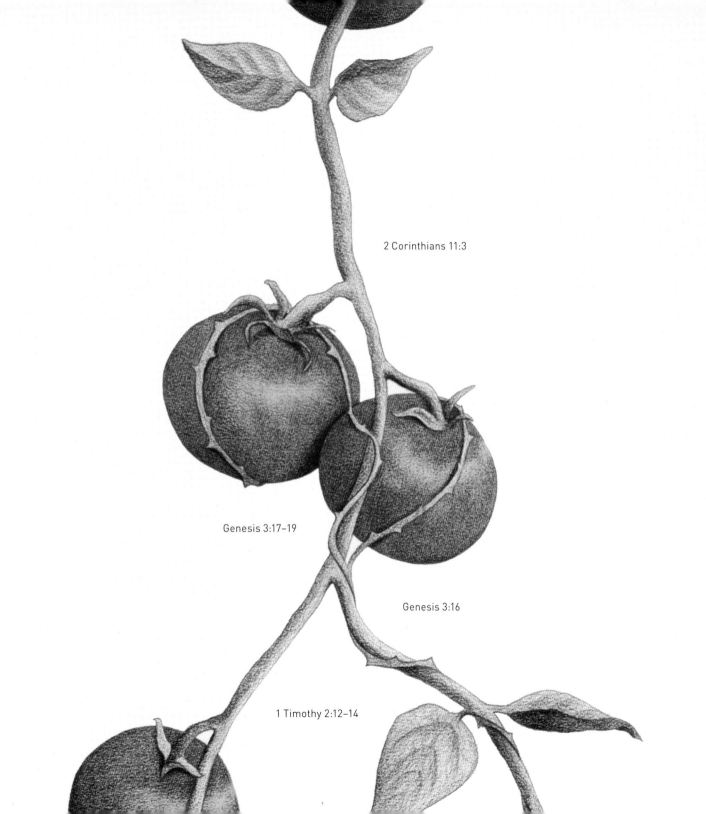

2 Corinthians 11:3

Genesis 3:17–19

Genesis 3:16

1 Timothy 2:12–14

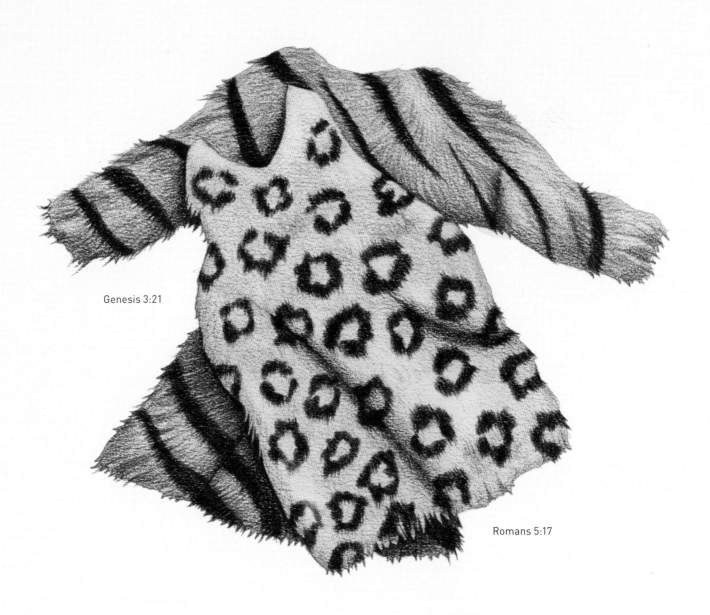

Genesis 3:21

Romans 5:17

17. God's Promise of Salvation

Even though his judgment was sad and hard, God still gave Adam and Eve hope. God added a promise to the end of the serpent's curse. The promise was that one day a son of Adam and Eve would fight the serpent. The serpent would strike at his heel but the son would defeat the serpent by crushing his head. From that day on, each son born to Adam and Eve gave them hope that he would be the savior God had promised.

Before sending Adam and Eve out of the garden, God made clothes for them out of the skin of an animal. Because they sinned and were now ashamed of being naked, an animal had to die so that they could have clothes to cover up. This might be hard to understand, but an animal skin covering Adam and Eve's nakedness is a picture of how God would bring salvation to his people through Jesus. Jesus shed his blood on the cross, so that our sins could be "covered." That means because of Jesus's death for us, God doesn't see our sins. He only sees Jesus's perfect life. But we are getting ahead of ourselves! Just remember that although it looked like Satan won in the garden, God had a plan to defeat Satan. And God's plan never fails!

For the wages of sin is death, but the free gift of God is eternal life in Christ Jesus our Lord.

ROMANS 6:23

18. God Sent Adam and Eve out of the Garden

As sinners, Adam and Eve could no longer remain with God in the garden. The things they enjoyed, like seeing God face-to-face, came to an end when they disobeyed his command. Adam and Eve could not be allowed to eat of the tree of life and live forever. So the Lord sent them from the garden and placed a cherubim and a flaming sword to guard the way to the tree of life so that they could never return.

Though God made them leave the garden, he did not send them totally away from him into hell. For God so loved the world that he planned to send his one and only Son, so that whoever would believe in him would not die but enjoy life forever. One day God would restore his creation and once again the tree of life would grow.

For as in
Adam all die,
so also in
Christ shall
all be made alive.
1 CORINTHIANS 15:22

Genesis 3:22–24

Revelation 22:2

John 3:16

Genesis 11:1–9

Genesis 6:5–7

Genesis 8:20–22

Genesis 6:11–13

19. Sin Spreads like a Disease

Sin grows and spreads, just like some diseases grow and spread, infecting one person after another. Adam and Eve's one sin brought all kinds of sins into the world. It started with their own children when their son Cain got so jealous and angry that he killed his brother Abel.

Sin is the kind of disease that always gets worse. As the years passed, sin got so bad that God sent a massive flood to clean up the whole world. But God had promised Adam and Eve that one of their descendants would defeat Satan. So God saved Noah and his family from the flood by having Noah build an ark.

But after the flood, it was obvious that sin had survived because Noah and his children were still doing things their way instead of God's way. Although the flood wiped out a world of evil, it could not stop sin from growing and spreading once again. The flood didn't destroy sin because sin lived inside the hearts of Noah and his family. Sin is inside us too. God's plan was to clean people from the inside. It took many centuries for his plan to be worked out. In the meantime, God promised to never again destroy the world with water and marked his promise with a rainbow.

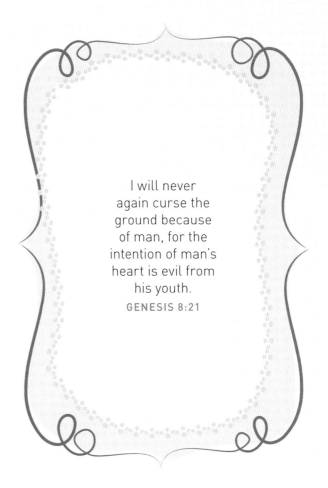

I will never again curse the ground because of man, for the intention of man's heart is evil from his youth.
GENESIS 8:21

The Ology of the Promise and the Law

Genesis 35:10

Hebrews 11:1, 8

Genesis 28:10–16

Isaiah 43:1–3

20. God Makes a Promise

God chose one of Noah's descendants, Abraham, to be the father of a nation that would belong to God. God called Abraham to leave his home in the city of Ur and take his wife, Sarah, to the land of Canaan. Once they arrived there, God promised the childless couple that from their family would come more children than there are stars in the sky and grains of sand on the seashore. They wouldn't just have a big family, one of their far off great-grandchildren would bring blessing to all the nations of earth. This child would save the world from sin and death.

God's promise was hard to believe because Abraham and Sarah were very old and had never had even one child. But they did believe God's promise. This is what it means to live by faith. Even before Jesus was born, those who believed in the promise of a Savior were accepted into God's family. By faith, when Sarah was ninety, she gave birth to a son, Isaac.

Eventually Isaac grew up, married, and had twin sons. God chose the younger, Jacob, to carry on the line of Abraham and be part of the fulfillment of God's promise. God gave Jacob the name Israel. Israel had twelve sons, who became the heads of the twelve tribes of Israel.

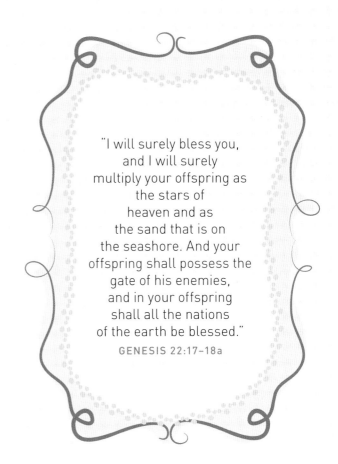

"I will surely bless you, and I will surely multiply your offspring as the stars of heaven and as the sand that is on the seashore. And your offspring shall possess the gate of his enemies, and in your offspring shall all the nations of the earth be blessed."
GENESIS 22:17–18a

21. God Keeps His Promise

When a famine threatened to destroy his family, Israel moved them to Egypt where God blessed them with many children. After a few hundred years, there were thousands of Israel's descendants living in Egypt. The Egyptians, worried that they might take over their country, forced the Israelites (or Hebrews) to become their slaves. But God, who always keeps his promises, hadn't forgotten his people or the promise he had made to them. He heard their cry for help and sent Moses to deliver them from slavery and lead them out of Egypt. God sent ten plagues to force Pharaoh, Egypt's king, to let the Israelites leave Egypt.

The last plague was the worst. God killed all the firstborn sons of Egypt. But he spared the Hebrews by telling them to paint the doorposts of their homes with the blood of a perfect lamb. When the angel of death saw the blood, he passed over them so that none of the Israelites were killed. After that, every year the people of Israel remembered how God delivered them from death through the blood of a lamb by celebrating a meal called Passover. One day God would send a different kind of lamb—"the Lamb of God who takes away the sin of the world"—to deliver his people from eternal death.

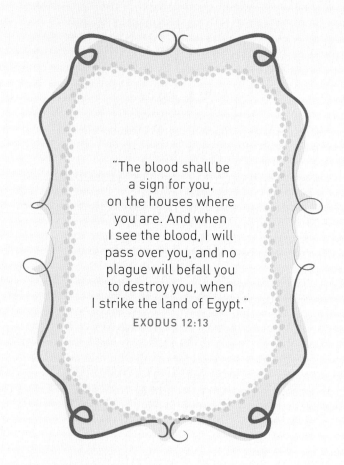

"The blood shall be a sign for you, on the houses where you are. And when I see the blood, I will pass over you, and no plague will befall you to destroy you, when I strike the land of Egypt."

EXODUS 12:13

Acts 7:30–34

Exodus 7:3–5

Exodus 3:10–12

Exodus 2:24

Exodus 1:8–13

Exodus 13:21–22

Deuteronomy 7:6

Hebrews 11:29

Exodus 17:3

Exodus 14:5–29

God led his people in a pillar of cloud by day and a pillar of fire by night. Although Pharaoh at first allowed Israel to leave Egypt, he changed his mind and chased them, trapping them at the Red Sea. But God opened the Red Sea and led them to safety, holding back the Egyptians with the great pillar of cloud. Once the people of Israel were safe on the other side, God allowed Pharaoh to chase them into the sea, where God sent the waters back over them, destroying the Egyptian army.

God lived among his people during their journey to the promised land of Canaan. When they were hungry, God fed them manna; when they were thirsty, he gave them water. But even though the Israelites were free from slavery to the Egyptians, they were still slaves to sin. They still wanted to go their own way. They complained about everything, and they didn't listen to Moses, the leader God gave them. Wanting his people to know how to love him and love others, God gave them laws. God's laws showed Israel how to love God, love people, and pointed out when they were going in the wrong direction.

With a strong hand
and an outstretched arm,
for his steadfast love
endures forever; to him who
divided the Red Sea in two,
for his steadfast
love endures forever;
and made Israel pass
through the midst of it, for
his steadfast love endures
forever; but overthrew
Pharaoh and his host in the
Red Sea, for his steadfast
love endures forever.

PSALM 136:12–15

22. The Ten Commandments of God

Speed limit signs are posted on highways to give drivers the rules of the road. If you drive faster than the speed limit, you are breaking the law. Speed laws keep us safe. Seat belt laws tell us to buckle up, forcing us to sit in our seats instead of playing on the car floor, but using seat belts saves us from injury in a crash. God's laws too are meant to protect us from the harm and the bad consequences of sin.

After leading Israel out of Egypt, God gave them the Ten Commandments to teach them the right way to love God and people. The first four commandments are about loving and worshiping God; the last six are about loving people.

I long for your salvation, O Lord, and your law is my delight.

PSALM 119:174

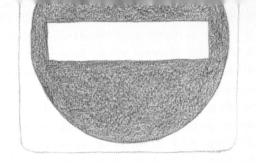

WAY

SPEED
LIMIT
35

John 13:34

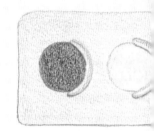

STOP

YIELD

Exodus 20:1–17

DEAD

1 John 3:15

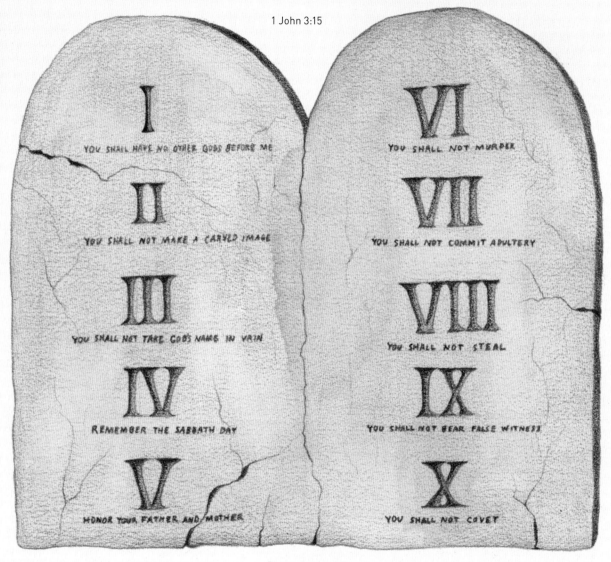

Matthew 5:22   Deuteronomy 6:5   Deuteronomy 5:7–22

Here are the Ten Commandments, which God spoke to Moses (you can read them for yourself in Exodus 20):

1. "You shall have no other gods before me" (verse 3).
2. "You shall not make for yourself a carved image, or any likeness of anything that is in heaven above, or that is in the earth beneath, or that is in the water under the earth" (verse 4).
3. "You shall not take the name of the LORD your God in vain" (verse 7).
4. "Remember the Sabbath day, to keep it holy. Six days you shall labor, and do all your work, but the seventh day is a Sabbath to the LORD your God" (verses 8–10a).
5. "Honor your father and your mother, that your days may be long in the land that the LORD your God is giving you" (verse 12).
6. "You shall not murder" (verse 13).
7. "You shall not commit adultery" (verse 14).
8. "You shall not steal" (verse 15).
9. "You shall not bear false witness against your neighbor" (verse 16).
10. "You shall not covet your neighbor's house; you shall not covet your neighbor's wife, or his male servant, or his female servant, or his ox, or his donkey, or anything that is your neighbor's" (verse 17).

"You shall love the Lord your God with all your heart and with all your soul and with all your strength and with all your mind, and your neighbor as yourself."

LUKE 10:27

23. Breaking One Law Breaks the Whole Law

The Ten Commandments are not like a set of ten china dishes, where if you chip or break one, you still have nine perfect plates. They are like one flawless plate, which has a border decorated with ten beautiful designs. Each design illustrates the law of love in a different way. Any crack, no matter where it is, ruins the whole plate. Should the plate crack across the words of the fifth commandment—"honor your father and mother"—the whole plate would be ruined.

So it is with the law: any sin breaks the whole law. Sin once and you are a sinner. God doesn't require us to be as good as we can be or to do the best job that we can. The holiness of God demands that we be perfect as our heavenly Father is perfect.

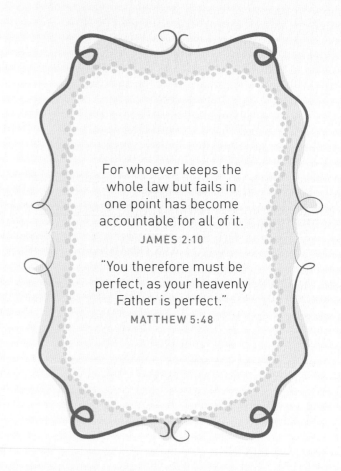

For whoever keeps the whole law but fails in one point has become accountable for all of it.
JAMES 2:10

"You therefore must be perfect, as your heavenly Father is perfect."
MATTHEW 5:48

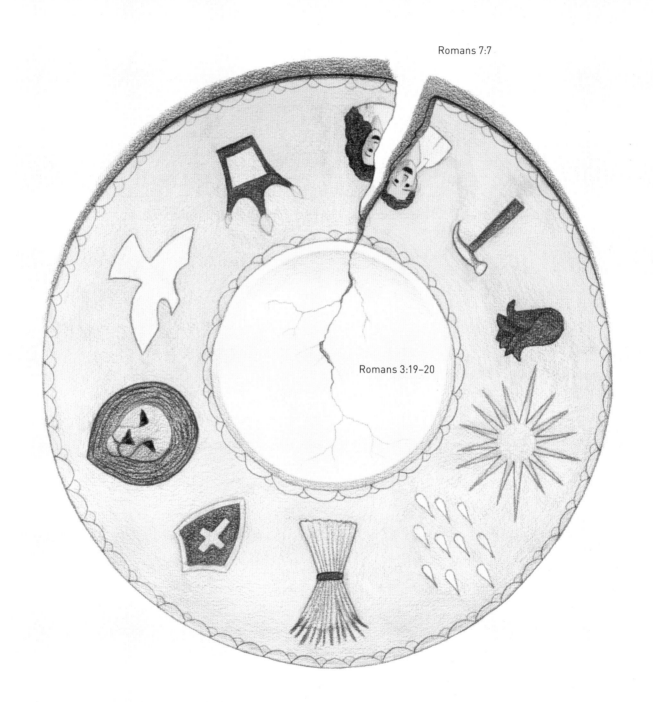

Romans 7:7

Romans 3:19–20

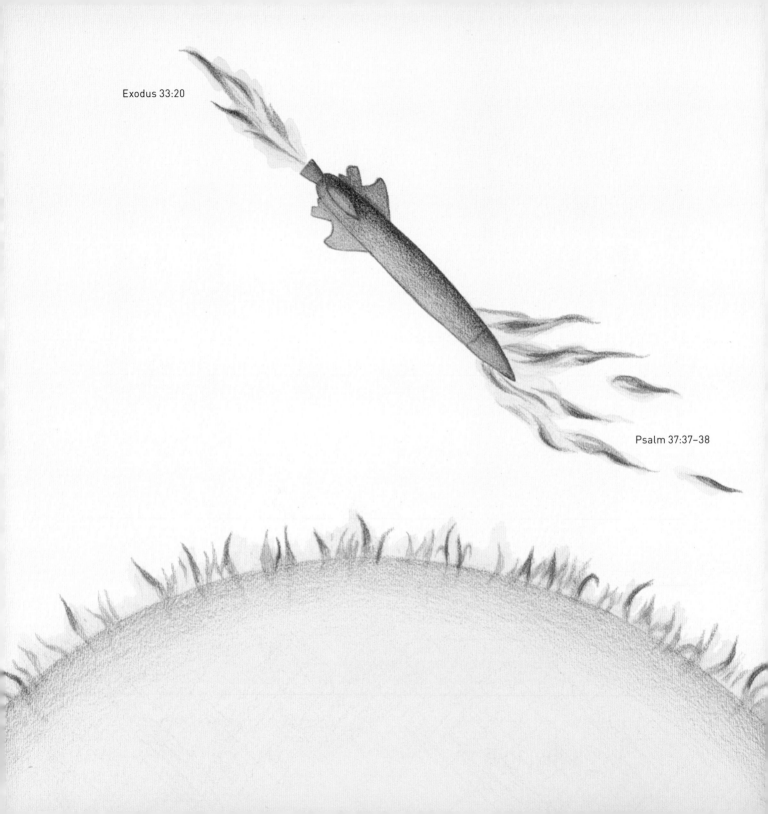

Exodus 33:20

Psalm 37:37–38

24. God's Holiness Cannot Be in the Same Place as Sin

Is it possible to get close enough to the sun to scoop out a sample to bring home in a jar? Of course not, the sun's surface is so hot it would burn you up before you even got close. While we know we can't touch the sun, a lot of folks don't understand that God's holy light—his glory and holiness—shines brighter than the sun. Just like we can't touch the sun, sinful people, still under judgment, can't get near to our holy God.

God is all-powerful and perfect in every way. When the angels worship him, they cry, "Holy, holy, holy is the Lord of hosts; the whole earth is full of his glory!" (Isaiah 6:3). Sin, on the other hand, is full of darkness and evil. God's pure holiness, like a giant solar flare, consumes sin and throws it far away from him. When Moses stood on Mount Sinai to receive the Ten Commandments, God warned the people to stay back. While Moses and a group of elders had special permission to come close to God, God said anyone else who even touched the edge of the mountain would die (Exodus 19:12). That is why sinful people cannot be near God until they have their sins washed away.

Our God is a consuming fire.
HEBREWS 12:29

The sinners in Zion are afraid; trembling has seized the godless: "Who among us can dwell with the consuming fire?"
ISAIAH 33:14a

Some people think that God won't care about their sins because they've tried hard to be good. But what they don't understand is that God's holiness and sin can't be near each other. Just as a lamp gets rid of the darkness in a room at night, so the light of God's holiness sends away anyone who has disobeyed God's law. Sin and God's holiness can't be in the same place at the same time. Sadly, we aren't able to get rid of our sins on our own.

The law does a great job of showing us the right way to live, but it can't change us—it can't take away even one sin. The law just keeps pointing out our faults, like a teacher shaking his finger at a disobedient student. But God always knew that the law couldn't save us. By showing us exactly what it means to love God and love others, the law helps us see how much we need saving and how far short we fall. When Jesus explained the law, he set the bar even higher because he said we must be perfect not only in what we do, but even in what we think! That makes it obvious that we need help from outside ourselves. We need a Savior who can keep the law *and* save us from the death that sin brings. We need Jesus, the Lamb of God, who takes away the sin of the world.

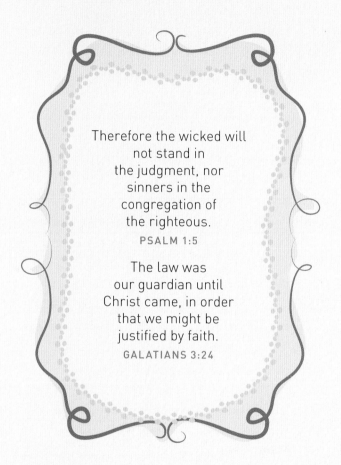

Therefore the wicked will not stand in the judgment, nor sinners in the congregation of the righteous.
PSALM 1:5

The law was our guardian until Christ came, in order that we might be justified by faith.
GALATIANS 3:24

Acts 3:19

Hebrews 9:27

Matthew 25:46

John 1:29

Leviticus 4:32–35

Leviticus 4:4

Leviticus 3:2

Leviticus 17:11

Leviticus 1:4

25. God Gave a Way to Cover Sin

While Moses was on Mount Sinai receiving God's law from God himself, the Israelites, camped at the foot of the mountain, were already breaking God's law by worshiping an idol. Rather than destroying his people then and there, God provided a way for the people to get rid of their sin. God gave his plan the name *atonement*, which means to cover over. God's plan involved killing an animal instead of the person who sinned.

Killing animals might seem like a harsh way to handle sin, but God wanted to send an important message: Everyone who sins owes God a life. Remember God's hard and fast rule that sin brings death? Someone has to pay for sin. Either we pay with our life, or someone else takes our place. There is no other way.

Indeed, under the law almost everything is purified with blood, and without the shedding of blood there is no forgiveness of sins.

HEBREWS 9:22

26. Jesus Is the Sacrifice We Need

Can the death of an animal really pay for someone's sin? Animals aren't like us at all; plus, how many animals would you have to sacrifice to atone for your sins? Every time you lied to your mom or hit your brother or sister, an animal would have to die. But we don't need to sacrifice animals for each of our sins anymore; God fulfilled his promise and sent his Son, Jesus, to obey the law completely and die as the perfect, spotless Lamb of God.

The sacrifice of Jesus on the cross is very different from an animal sacrifice. The animal sacrifices covered sin, but did not take it away. They were a little like cleaning your room by shoving everything under the bed. The bed covers the mess but the mess is still there. That is why animals had to be sacrificed again and again and again. But Jesus's sacrifice on the cross was good once and for all. His death restores order to the messy room that is our sin-stained heart.

For it is impossible for the blood of bulls and goats to take away sins.
HEBREWS 10:4

"Come now, let us reason together, says the Lord: though your sins are like scarlet, they shall be as white as snow."
ISAIAH 1:18a

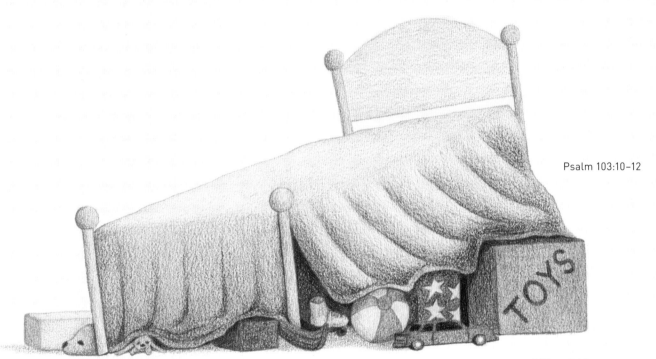

Psalm 103:10–12

Isaiah 53:5–6

1 Kings 8:63

The Ology
of Christ

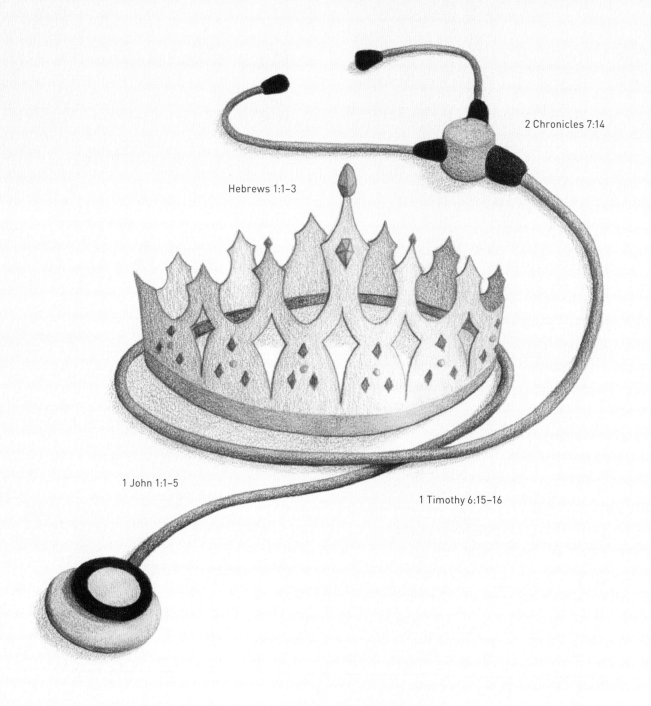

2 Chronicles 7:14

Hebrews 1:1–3

1 John 1:1–5

1 Timothy 6:15–16

27. The Son of God Comes to Earth

Imagine a wise king, educated in law, medicine, and history, dressed in royal robes and a crown, and sitting on a throne. Everyone who comes before him bows low. Now picture a day when a deadly plague infects the people of his country. No doctor can find a cure for it; in fact, they too are dying. Out of love for his people, the king leaves his throne, takes off his crown, replaces his royal robes with a simple cloak, collects his doctor's bag, and goes out to heal his people. This is what King Jesus did for us.

Forever, the Son of God had lived in perfect love with the Father and the Holy Spirit. The angels worshiped the Father, Son, and Holy Spirit before the throne of God in a light-filled, joy-filled heaven. But one day, as sin spread like a disease through the earth, the glorious Son of God stepped off his throne. He set aside his glory in obedience to his Father's request to save his people. Because he loved the Father and his people, the Son of God humbled himself, took a body like ours, and brought healing to our sin-sick world.

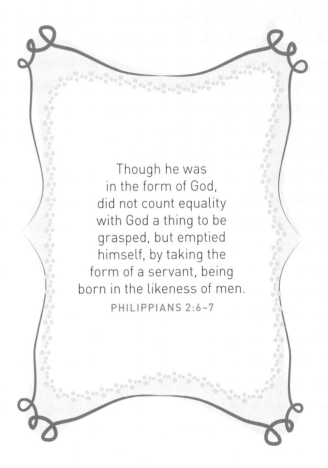

Though he was
in the form of God,
did not count equality
with God a thing to be
grasped, but emptied
himself, by taking the
form of a servant, being
born in the likeness of men.

PHILIPPIANS 2:6–7

When the right time had come, the Father sent the angel Gabriel to announce to Mary, a special young woman, that she would be the mother of his Son. Mary was a far-off ancestor of Israel's greatest king, David. Ever since the fall, God's people struggled with sin. But now it was time for the Savior to come and save God's people from the curse that first began when Adam and Eve disobeyed.

When Gabriel appeared to her and told her that she would have a child by the power of the Holy Spirit, she was afraid (everyone who meets an angel is pretty scared!). She was also confused. How was it possible to have a child without a husband? But Gabriel told her that the power of God would come upon her and that the son she would have would be called Jesus.

Then he told her a little bit about the amazing child she would have: he would be the Son of the Most High and the new king of Israel. Even though this was a lot to take in, Mary said, "Let it be to me as you have said" (see Luke 1:38). What made Mary special was her faith and trust in God.

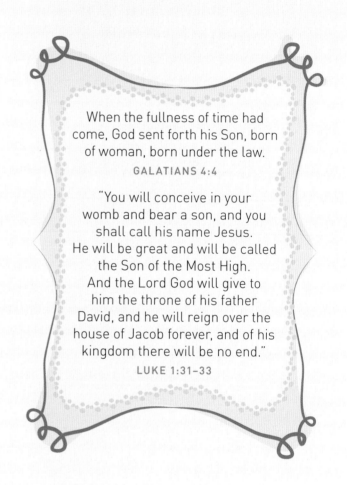

When the fullness of time had come, God sent forth his Son, born of woman, born under the law.
GALATIANS 4:4

"You will conceive in your womb and bear a son, and you shall call his name Jesus. He will be great and will be called the Son of the Most High. And the Lord God will give to him the throne of his father David, and he will reign over the house of Jacob forever, and of his kingdom there will be no end."
LUKE 1:31–33

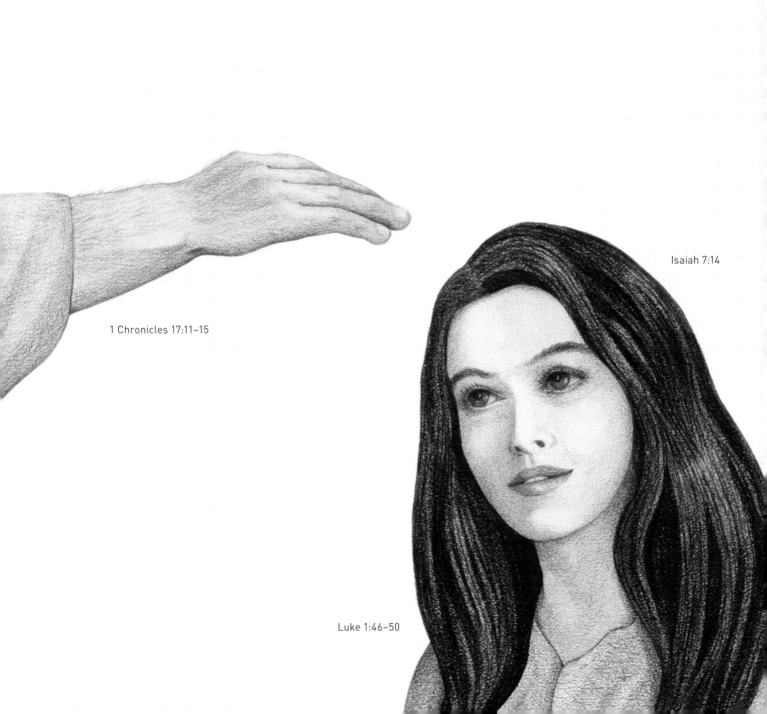

1 Chronicles 17:11–15

Isaiah 7:14

Luke 1:46–50

Isaiah 33:22

Matthew 1:18–25

28. The Son Stepped off His Throne

The angels of heaven watched with wonder as the Son of God stepped off his throne and came down to earth as a baby to grow inside the young woman Mary.

Mary didn't have to raise this amazing child by herself. God had already given her Joseph, a man she was getting ready to marry. But Mary was worried about how to explain to Joseph that she was pregnant with God's child. Just as Mary feared, Joseph was confused when she told him that God had caused a child to grow inside her.

But God took care of that and sent an angel to Joseph in a dream to explain that the baby boy in Mary's womb was indeed from the Holy Spirit. The angel then instructed Joseph to name the child Jesus, for he would save his people from their sins.

Surely the arm of the
LORD is not too short to save,
nor his ear too dull to hear.
ISAIAH 59:1 NIV

"Behold, the virgin shall conceive and bear a son, and they shall call his name Immanuel" (which means, God with us).
MATTHEW 1:23

Nine months after the angel's visit to Mary, the Son of God was born in a humble stable in Joseph's hometown of Bethlehem. All of heaven held its breath, waiting as an angel announced Christ's birth to shepherds guarding their sheep that special night. After the announcement, the angels exploded in a chorus of joy that rang out over the glory-lit hillside near Bethlehem, "Glory to God in the highest and peace on earth."

The shepherds were dumbfounded. One minute they were sleepily watching their sheep, and the next they were watching a concert from heaven! What could this all mean? They could barely take in the news that the promised Savior had been born, but they knew they had to go see for themselves. So, leaving their sheep, they hurried to the manger where the newborn Savior lay.

And the angel said to them, "Fear not, for behold, I bring you good news of great joy that will be for all the people. For unto you is born this day in the city of David a Savior, who is Christ the Lord. And this will be a sign for you: you will find a baby wrapped in swaddling cloths and lying in a manger."

LUKE 2:10–12

Isaiah 9:6

Luke 1:46–50

Luke 2:13–14

Luke 2:7

Micah 5:2

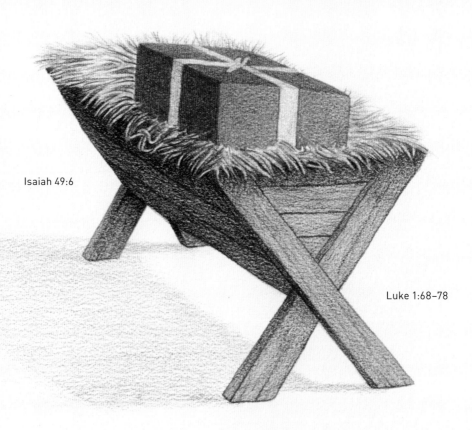

Isaiah 49:6

Luke 1:68–78

We celebrate Jesus's birth on December 25 by giving and getting Christmas gifts. As Christmas nears, we wait excitedly for our gifts. When the day finally arrives we have fun unwrapping our presents. Exchanging gifts is a fun Christmas tradition, but did you know it was God who started the giving at Christmas? In fact, giving is what Christmas is all about.

More than two thousand years ago, with the birth of Jesus, God the Father gave the first and best Christmas present of all time. He gave to us his one and only Son. The angels knew the day was coming and they couldn't wait to shout and sing God's praises. The prophets knew and passed on clues so that Israel would also look forward to the day their Savior would be born. The wise men knew and traveled a great distance with their own gifts for the young King. So each year when you get excited about Christmas and presents, remember God's gift of Jesus, where all the excitement of Christmas and presents began.

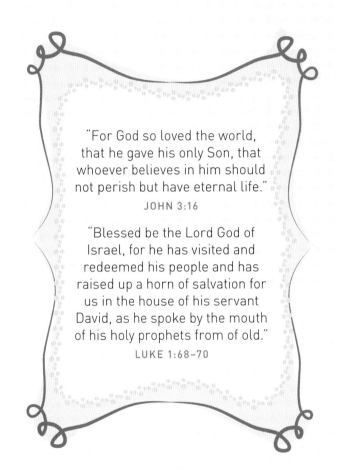

"For God so loved the world, that he gave his only Son, that whoever believes in him should not perish but have eternal life."
JOHN 3:16

"Blessed be the Lord God of Israel, for he has visited and redeemed his people and has raised up a horn of salvation for us in the house of his servant David, as he spoke by the mouth of his holy prophets from of old."
LUKE 1:68–70

29. Jesus Always Loved God and People

God's Son has always loved his Father and the people he created in his image. From the time he was born, Jesus never sinned, even once. He obeyed God the Father by obeying his parents and doing everything they told him to do. He never whined or complained when it was time to go to bed. He didn't grab other children's toys or lie about anything. He helped around the home, and he worked hard at his studies and with his earthly father Joseph in his carpenter's shop.

Imagine if Jesus had a chore chart to show how well he obeyed and did his chores. He would have check marks next to each and every chore! But even more amazing, he wasn't just good on the outside. He was good through and through. Even his thoughts were kind and loving.

Once when Jesus was twelve years old, his parents were upset because they didn't know where he was. But even then he didn't do anything wrong, and eventually they found him in the temple learning about God among the teachers. Jesus listened to his parents; and the Bible tells us that as he got older he grew in wisdom, stature, and favor with God and man. Jesus knew, in order to save us from our sin, he would have to obey in all things perfectly and that is just what he did.

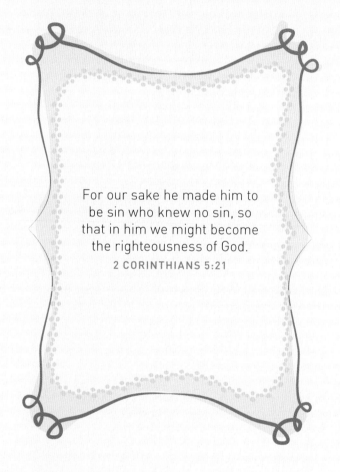

For our sake he made him to be sin who knew no sin, so that in him we might become the righteousness of God.

2 CORINTHIANS 5:21

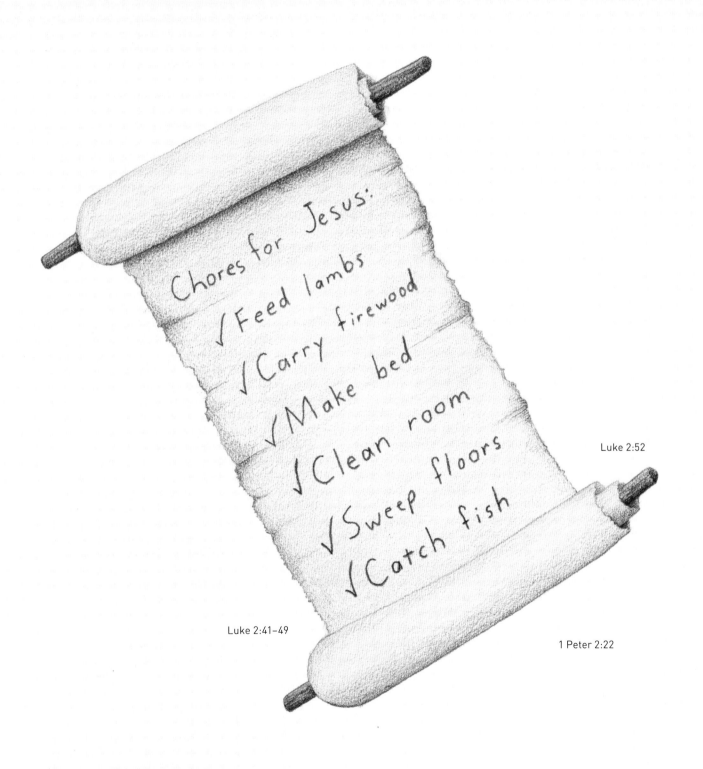

Luke 2:52

Luke 2:41–49

1 Peter 2:22

James 4:7

Luke 11:1–4

1 Corinthians 10:13

Hebrews 2:18

Matthew 4:1–11

When Jesus was grown up, just before his mission for God began, Satan (as he had with Adam and Eve) tried to get Jesus to sin—to stop listening to God and listen to him instead. If Jesus listened to Satan, his mission on earth to save his people from their sins would be over before it even started.

Satan found Jesus when he was weak and hungry, because he hadn't eaten for forty days. Unlike Adam and Eve whom Satan tempted while they lived in a beautiful garden full of good things to eat, Jesus was starving and in a desert when Satan appeared to him.

Instead of tempting Jesus once as he had Adam and Eve, Satan tempted Jesus three times. First, Satan tried to get Jesus to use his power to satisfy his hunger by turning stones into bread. Next, Satan told Jesus to throw himself off the top of the temple to prove that God would save him. And, finally, Satan offered Jesus the world to rule if only Jesus would worship him. Unlike Adam who had given in to Satan's temptations, Jesus resisted the enemy's lies by speaking the truth of God's Word. After Satan's third attempt, he fled at Jesus's command. Then angels came and cared for Jesus.

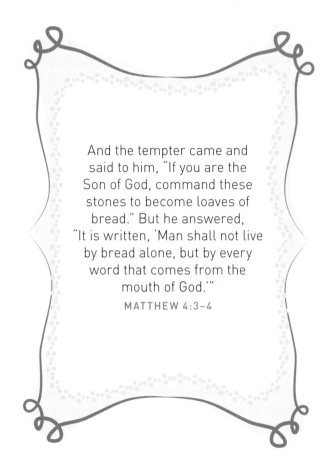

And the tempter came and said to him, "If you are the Son of God, command these stones to become loaves of bread." But he answered, "It is written, 'Man shall not live by bread alone, but by every word that comes from the mouth of God.'"

MATTHEW 4:3-4

30. Jesus Is Completely Human

You have already learned that Jesus is God. He is the second person of the Trinity—the Son of God who left his throne in heaven to come to earth to save his people. But Jesus was also a real person whom you could see and touch. If you had lived in those days, you could have shaken his hand, or joined him for a meal. As a baby, Jesus had to learn to talk and walk and needed to be fed and cared for like any young child. As God, Jesus was all-knowing, but as a young man he had to learn and study God's Word.

Jesus experienced all of the troubles and challenges that life brings. Just like us, he got hungry, thirsty, and tired. He felt sad when hard things happened and felt terrible pain and suffering on the cross before his death. But because of his great love for us, Jesus endured these trials and trusted God his Father through them all.

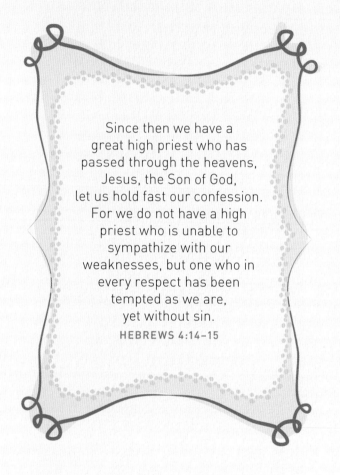

Since then we have a great high priest who has passed through the heavens, Jesus, the Son of God, let us hold fast our confession. For we do not have a high priest who is unable to sympathize with our weaknesses, but one who in every respect has been tempted as we are, yet without sin.

HEBREWS 4:14–15

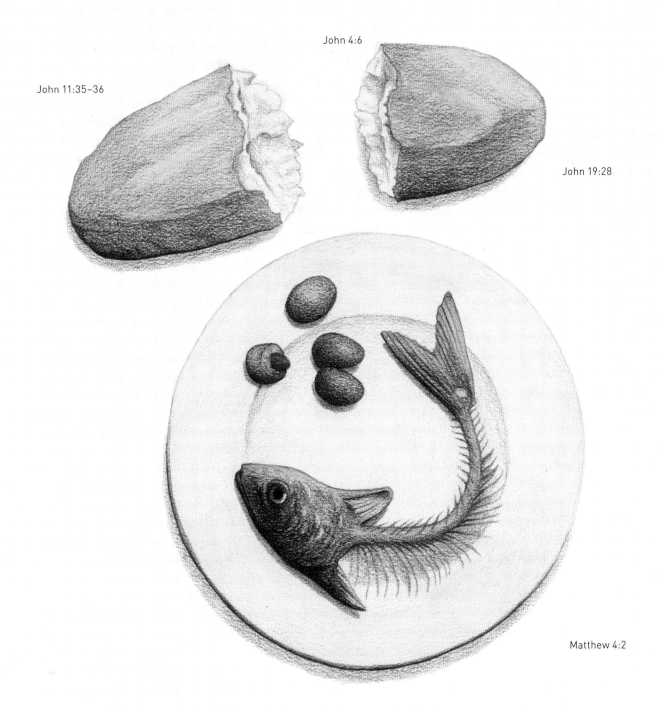

John 4:6

John 11:35–36

John 19:28

Matthew 4:2

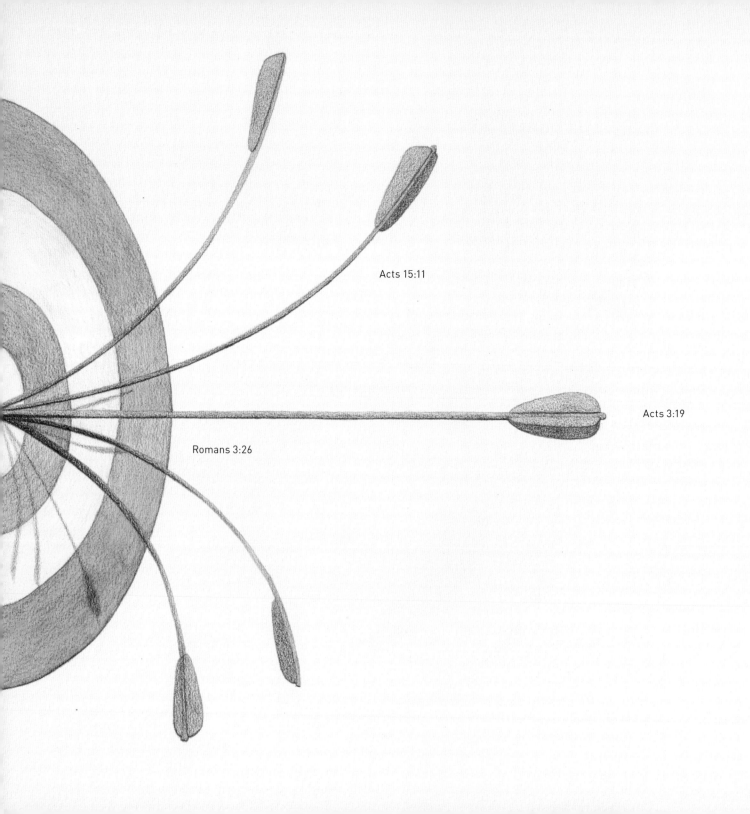

Acts 15:11

Acts 3:19

Romans 3:26

For a person to be perfect, he or she can't make even the smallest mistake, like an archer who hits the exact center of the target every single time. In spite of temptations and trials, Jesus obeyed God's law of love every minute of his entire life. The Bible calls this perfect obedience "righteousness." Jesus did what was perfectly right and loving all the time, every time. And that made Jesus different from every other person who ever lived, including you and me. Not only did Jesus stand up to Satan's temptations perfectly, but he also loved perfectly—he loved God with all his heart, soul, and mind, and he loved others as he loved himself.

The Bible calls Jesus "the second Adam." The first Adam failed to love God and brought sin and sorrow into our world. But because Jesus lived the life of obedience that Adam could not, he is able to offer his perfect life for our sins. Because he was righteous, he could trade his righteous life for our sinful one. This trade cost Jesus his life, but he has given it to us freely by his grace. This amazing trade is available to anyone who is willing to turn to Jesus and place their trust in him.

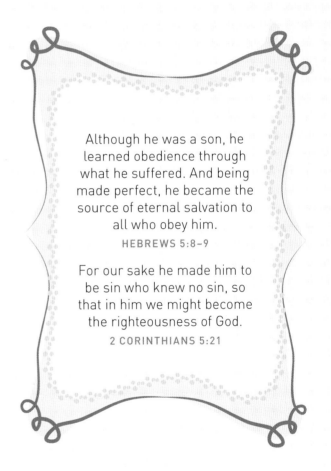

Although he was a son, he learned obedience through what he suffered. And being made perfect, he became the source of eternal salvation to all who obey him.

HEBREWS 5:8–9

For our sake he made him to be sin who knew no sin, so that in him we might become the righteousness of God.

2 CORINTHIANS 5:21

31. Jesus Is Completely God

While Jesus was fully human, he was also fully God and all-powerful. This means he could do things that only God can do. He could turn water into wine, and he could multiply a few fish and loaves of bread to feed a crowd of more than five thousand. Jesus could even walk on water. If you ever wonder if Jesus was really God, try walking on water the next time you go swimming!

Jesus healed all kinds of sicknesses: blindness, leprosy, fevers, shriveled hands, and epilepsy. He even made the lame walk and the deaf hear. Jesus stopped the wind and calmed the sea, and he set people free from evil spirits.

But the most amazing of his miracles was when Jesus demonstrated his power over death. Jesus brought back to life a widow's son, a little girl, and his friend Lazarus who had been dead four days. And finally, of course, on the third day after his own death, Jesus rose again from the dead. All of these miracles were meant to be signs that God had really come to earth to save his people. And the resurrection was THE sign that Jesus had finished the work of salvation.

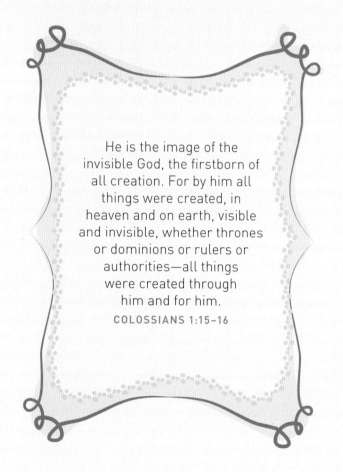

He is the image of the invisible God, the firstborn of all creation. For by him all things were created, in heaven and on earth, visible and invisible, whether thrones or dominions or rulers or authorities—all things were created through him and for him.
COLOSSIANS 1:15–16

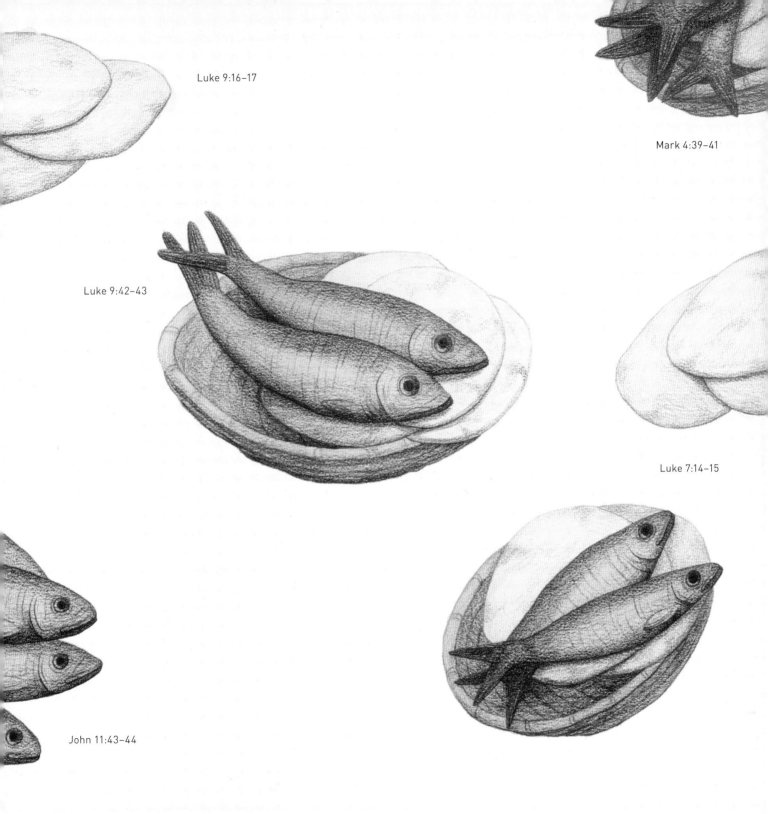

Luke 9:16–17

Mark 4:39–41

Luke 9:42–43

Luke 7:14–15

John 11:43–44

John 20:26–29

Mark 2:8

Matthew 8:29

Matthew 14:33

John 10:33

Jesus knew what the Pharisees were thinking about him even when they didn't say anything. And Jesus knew Judas was going to betray him long before he did. Today, by his Spirit, Jesus is present everywhere, for he said that wherever two or more people are gathered to pray in his name, he is with us.

When someone with the wrong number calls your phone, they often ask for someone you don't know. When that happens folks usually reply, "I'm sorry, there is no one here by that name. You have the wrong number." Imagine someone, thinking you are a plumber, asking you to come fix a leaky pipe. If you were not the plumber you would say, "I'm sorry, but you've got the wrong person."

But when demons called Jesus the Son of God, Jesus didn't say they had the wrong person. When the disciples worshiped Jesus after he walked on the water, Jesus didn't refuse their worship. After Jesus rose from the dead, when Thomas saw the nail marks on Jesus's hands and called him his Lord and his God, Jesus said that everyone who believes in him, as Thomas did, would be blessed. This means that if we believe that Jesus is God, we will also be blessed.

Thomas answered him,
"My Lord and my God!"
Jesus said to him,
"Have you believed
because you have seen me?
Blessed are those
who have not seen and
yet have believed."
JOHN 20:28–29

32. Jesus Died in Our Place

Dams hold back floodwaters during heavy rains. But if a dam bursts, and the water stored up rushes out all at once, it can wash a town away in minutes. From the time of Adam and Eve's first sin until the time of Jesus, God's judgment—his punishment—for everybody's sins was held back, just as a dam holds back floodwaters.

Out of his loving kindness and mercy, God held back his judgment for sin until the day when his only Son Jesus took the place of sinners on the cross. Jesus willingly received our punishment—all of God's stored-up wrath for our sin—as he became sin for us. As Jesus hung on the cross, God allowed the dam to burst and his wrath to pour out on his beloved Son. God's plan, from the very first sacrifice for sin, was to offer his Son as our substitute, to take our punishment.

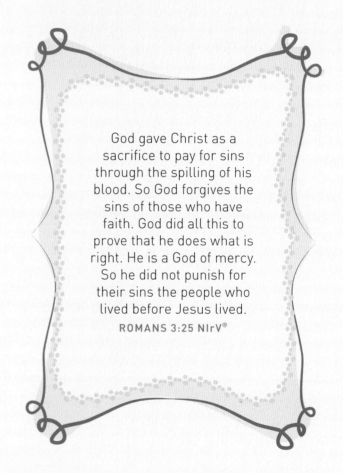

God gave Christ as a sacrifice to pay for sins through the spilling of his blood. So God forgives the sins of those who have faith. God did all this to prove that he does what is right. He is a God of mercy. So he did not punish for their sins the people who lived before Jesus lived.

ROMANS 3:25 NIrV®

1 John 4:10

1 Peter 3:18

2 Corinthians 5:21

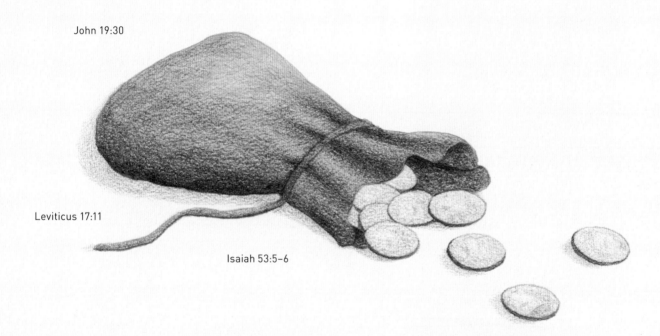

John 19:30

Leviticus 17:11

Isaiah 53:5–6

Taking our place on the cross meant that Jesus suffered in every way possible. He was betrayed by one of his close friends, Judas, for thirty silver coins. The leaders of his own Jewish community were the ones who plotted to kill him. When he was arrested, his closest friends scattered. One friend, Peter, even lied and said he did not know Jesus.

Jesus was mocked, crowned with painful thorns, and beaten terribly. He was forced to climb a rocky hill carrying a cross. At the top of the hill, Jesus was nailed to the cross by his hands and feet, and then the cross was pulled up for everyone to see.

But the mockery of the crowd and the pain of the nails could not compare with Jesus's suffering when God's wrath—God's anger for our sin—burst like a giant dam and flooded over him. We can't imagine the terrible suffering this must have meant for Jesus. With God's wrath completely poured out—with every sin paid for—Jesus said, "It is finished." Then he bowed his head and died. Jesus, the Lamb of God, had paid the penalty for our sin.

And going a little farther
he fell on his face
and prayed, saying,
"My Father, if it be possible,
let this cup pass from me;
nevertheless, not as I will,
but as you will."
MATTHEW 26:39

33. Jesus's Resurrection Defeated Death

After Jesus died, his body was taken off the cross by Joseph of Arimathea and Nicodemus. They wrapped his body in linen cloths with spices, laid him in a tomb cut out of the rock, and rolled a heavy stone in front of the entrance.

Afraid that Jesus's disciples would steal his body, the leaders of the Jewish people, with Pilate's permission, sealed the tomb and posted a guard. But no guard could stop the power of God. On the morning of the third day, a great earthquake rocked the earth as a shining angel of the Lord rolled the stone away from the tomb's entrance. The guards fell to the ground in fear.

When the first women arrived at the tomb, the angel greeted them with an amazing message. "I know you are looking for Jesus who was crucified," the angel said. "He is not here, for he has risen, just as he said." Then the angel instructed the women to go quickly and tell the disciples, "Jesus has risen from the dead and he will meet you in Galilee." The women ran to their friends with great joy to report the good news.

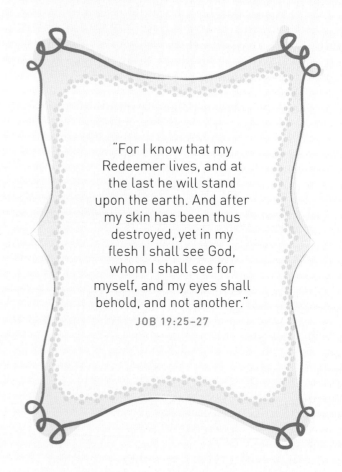

"For I know that my Redeemer lives, and at the last he will stand upon the earth. And after my skin has been thus destroyed, yet in my flesh I shall see God, whom I shall see for myself, and my eyes shall behold, and not another."

JOB 19:25–27

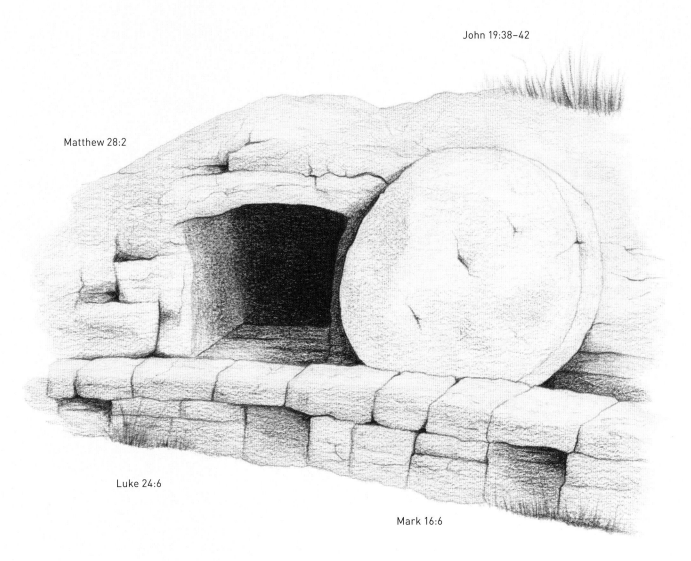

John 19:38–42

Matthew 28:2

Luke 24:6

Mark 16:6

Matthew 28:6

Acts 2:24–28

Romans 8:11

1 Corinthians 6:14

John 10:18

John 5:21

Romans 14:9

35. Jesus Sends His Disciples on a Mission

In banks, security cameras record everything that happens. If a thief comes in to rob the bank, everything they do is captured on the recording to play back for everyone to see. The bank tellers also become witnesses to the crime and can report the robbery to the police. A witness is a person who saw what happened, with his or her own eyes.

Wouldn't it be great if there had been video cameras back in Jesus's day to record everything he did? Then we could replay the recordings and watch Jesus healing the sick, teaching the people, and rising from the dead.

Even though video cameras were not invented yet, Jesus made sure there were witnesses to tell us what they saw with their own eyes. Jesus chose the twelve disciples to follow him wherever he went, hear everything he said, and see all that he did. After his resurrection, Jesus appeared to over five hundred people so that everyone would know he really rose again.

That which was from the beginning, which we have heard, which we have seen with our eyes, which we looked upon and have touched with our hands, concerning the word of life.

1 JOHN 1:1

One day after his resurrection Jesus appeared to his disciples and sat down to share a meal with them. Jesus helped them to understand how the Law, the Prophets, and the Psalms (what we now call the Old Testament) told about his suffering and rising from the dead hundreds of years before it all happened.

Then Jesus explained to the disciples that they were his witnesses because they had seen with their own eyes all that happened, especially his resurrection. He told them to go and tell everyone about him; Jesus wanted everyone to turn from their sins and trust in him. But before they could go, Jesus told them to wait in Jerusalem until they received the Holy Spirit who would give them the power to carry out their task.

Did you know that Jesus has sent you on a mission too? When you ask Jesus for forgiveness for your sins and follow him, you become a witness to how Jesus can save his people from sin. Now as Jesus's witness, you get to go and tell others that Jesus can save them from sin too.

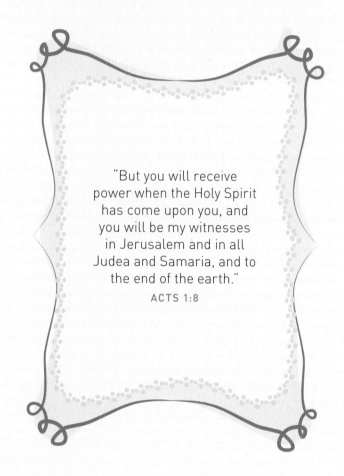

"But you will receive power when the Holy Spirit has come upon you, and you will be my witnesses in Jerusalem and in all Judea and Samaria, and to the end of the earth."

ACTS 1:8

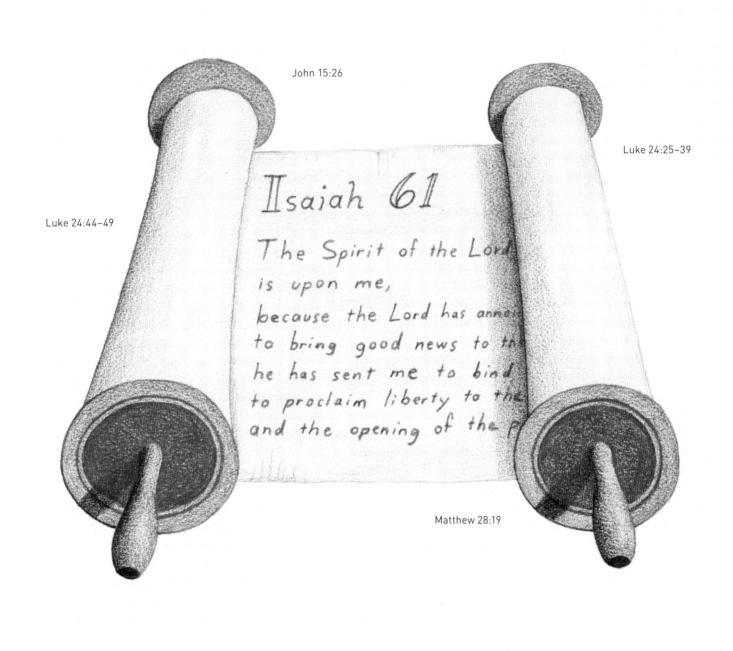

John 15:26

Luke 24:25–39

Luke 24:44–49

Isaiah 61

The Spirit of the Lord
is upon me,
because the Lord has anne
to bring good news to th
he has sent me to bind
to proclaim liberty to the
and the opening of the p

Matthew 28:19

The Ology
of the
Holy Spirit

Acts 1:4–8

John 14:26

John 15:26

John 14:17

36. Jesus Promised to Send the Holy Spirit

Did you ever need someone to help you move something that was too big for you to carry alone, like carrying a long ladder? It is so much better to ask for help, than to try and do it by yourself.

Following Jesus is too big a job for any of us to do by ourselves; that is why Jesus sent the Holy Spirit. The night of his arrest, Jesus told his disciples that soon he was going to leave them. The disciples were sad when they heard that, but Jesus said something surprising: he told them that it would actually be better for him to go away, because then he could send them the Holy Spirit to be their helper. The Holy Spirit lives inside each of Jesus's followers, helping us remember what Jesus taught and giving us the power to love others and say no to sin. Just like the disciples, we need the Spirit to help us too!

When Jesus lived on earth, he could only be in one place at a time. But after he went to heaven, by his Spirit, Jesus lives in each one of his people, helping us to remember everything Jesus said and giving us the power to live like Jesus! After Jesus rose from the dead, just before he went back to heaven, he told his disciples that the Holy Spirit would come to them in just a few days, and they would be his witnesses to tell the whole earth about him.

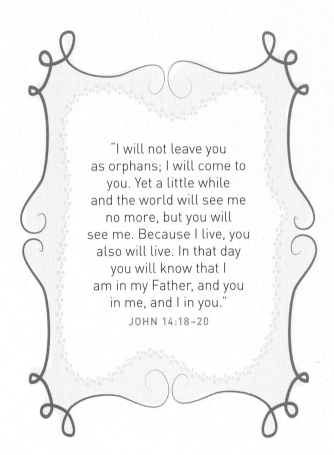

"I will not leave you as orphans; I will come to you. Yet a little while and the world will see me no more, but you will see me. Because I live, you also will live. In that day you will know that I am in my Father, and you in me, and I in you."

JOHN 14:18–20

37. The Spirit Arrives on Pentecost

When someone tells you that they sent you a gift, you often wonder when it will arrive. Did you ever wait by the window for a delivery to come? Sometimes when you have to wait a long time, you might even wonder if it really is going to come at all. Imagine how hard it was for Jesus's friends to wait for the Holy Spirit. Jesus said he would send him in a few days, but they didn't know what to look for.

But when the Holy Spirit came, everyone knew something amazing was happening. A loud, powerful wind blew through the room; and tongues of fire appeared over the heads of Jesus's followers as each of them were filled with the Holy Spirit and began to praise God in other languages. There was a large crowd from many different countries gathered in Jerusalem for the feast of Pentecost. Amazingly, each person heard Jesus's followers praising God in their own language. For the first time since the tower of Babel where, because of sin, God had separated people by giving them different languages, people who spoke different languages were united again. This was the beginning of God's Spirit bringing people from all over the world into God's family, keeping God's promise to bless all the nations through him.

"And it shall come to pass afterward, that I will pour out my Spirit on all flesh; your sons and your daughters shall prophesy, your old men shall dream dreams, and your young men shall see visions."

JOEL 2:28

Acts 2:14–17

Acts 2:1–4

Isaiah 44:3

John 16:7

Ephesians 2:18

1 Corinthians 6:19

John 16:12–14

38. The Holy Spirit: God's Best Gift

To the amazement of the crowd, Peter, filled with the Holy Spirit, shouted out the good news that Jesus was not dead, but alive forever and ready to forgive the sins of all who trusted in him. What a difference the Holy Spirit made in Peter! Remember how he said he didn't even know Jesus the night Jesus was arrested? Now he bravely preached to a huge crowd.

At first the people listening thought maybe Jesus's disciples were drunk! But Peter explained that they were filled with the Holy Spirit. He told the crowd if they turned away from their sin and believed in Jesus they could be filled with the Holy Spirit too! Peter said that the promise of the Holy Spirit was for them, for their children, and for everyone the Lord calls into his family. When Peter finished talking, his hearers were "cut to the heart"—deep inside they understood that they were sinners who needed a Savior. That's what Jesus had promised the Holy Spirit would do—he would come to those whom God was calling and show them their sin and how much they needed Jesus. That day three thousand people believed and were added to the first church.

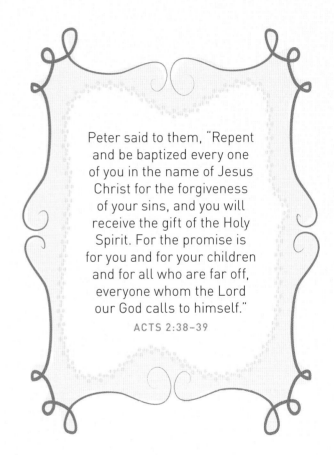

Peter said to them, "Repent and be baptized every one of you in the name of Jesus Christ for the forgiveness of your sins, and you will receive the gift of the Holy Spirit. For the promise is for you and for your children and for all who are far off, everyone whom the Lord our God calls to himself."

ACTS 2:38–39

Imagine that your parents promised you a bike for Christmas. But they didn't just promise it to you, they brought you to the store, let you pick out the bike you wanted, and then gave the store some money, as a deposit, to hold that exact bike until Christmas. Then you would really know that you were getting that bike! In the same way, the gift of the Holy Spirit living inside of us is our deposit and guarantee that we will go to heaven to be with Jesus. The Bible tells us we can sense his presence and know he is with us.

How do we know the Spirit lives in us? Well, only the Holy Spirit can help us turn away from our sin and believe in Jesus. The Holy Spirit is the one who shows us that we are sinners who need Jesus. Once we come to Jesus, he makes us more like Jesus. Because of the Spirit we have Jesus's power to love even really annoying people and to share the good news about Jesus with others. We can tell that the Holy Spirit is inside because we think and do things that are different. And best of all, down deep inside, even though we still sin, we want to follow God and get to know him better. Once we have the Holy Spirit, no one can take him away from us.

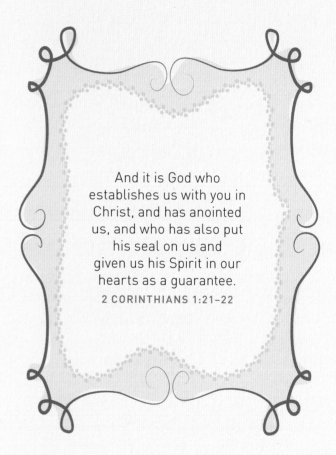

And it is God who establishes us with you in Christ, and has anointed us, and who has also put his seal on us and given us his Spirit in our hearts as a guarantee.

2 CORINTHIANS 1:21–22

John 16:8–11

Acts 2:16–18

John 14:16

Ephesians 1:14

Luke 11:12–13

The Ology
of Adoption
into God's
Family

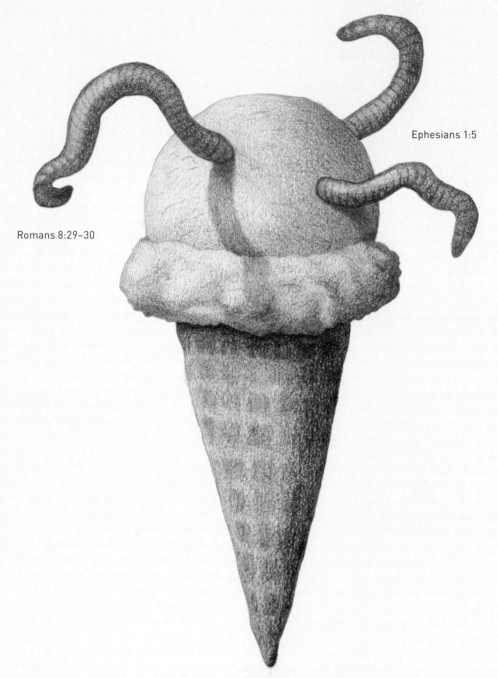

Romans 8:29–30

Ephesians 1:5

1 Peter 2:9

39. Chosen

Imagine going to an ice cream parlor on a hot day to buy an ice cream cone. The hardest part is trying to decide which flavor to get.

Some people love chocolate and will only choose ice cream with chocolate in it. Others enjoy big, chewy chunks of candy in their ice cream. But what if you went into an ice cream shop and none of the flavors had any appeal. Imagine flavors like stinky sneaker, mildew swirl, and earthworm chunk? You would most likely leave the shop without getting anything.

We choose ice cream that tastes good. But when God chose us to be a part of his family, we were yucky, spoiled sinners—not one of us was good. God didn't choose us because he needed us or because we had some special quality, God chose us while we were still sinners, just because he decided to love us.

He chose us in him before the foundation of the world, that we should be holy and blameless before him.
EPHESIANS 1:4

After Adam and Eve sinned, they hid from God. We do the same thing when we sin—we try to hide from God and get as far away as we can. Without God's help, no one would turn to him. We are all like runaway trains, speeding away from God toward a terrible crash. But because of his love and not because of anything we have done, God chose to save some who ran away.

Even before creating the world, God chose his children. He knew Adam and Eve would sin, and he planned before creation to send his only Son to rescue his people from sin and death.

It's good news that God chooses us, because sadly, without the Spirit changing our minds, we would never choose him! The Bible even says that we were "dead" in our sin and the Spirit has to first make us alive before we believe! Apart from God, we are helpless to choose him. We don't even like God until he breathes life into us, opening our eyes to see him. Only then, alive in Christ, do we choose to follow God and live for him.

But God, being rich in mercy, because of the great love with which he loved us, even when we were dead in our trespasses, made us alive together with Christ—by grace you have been saved.

EPHESIANS 2:4–5

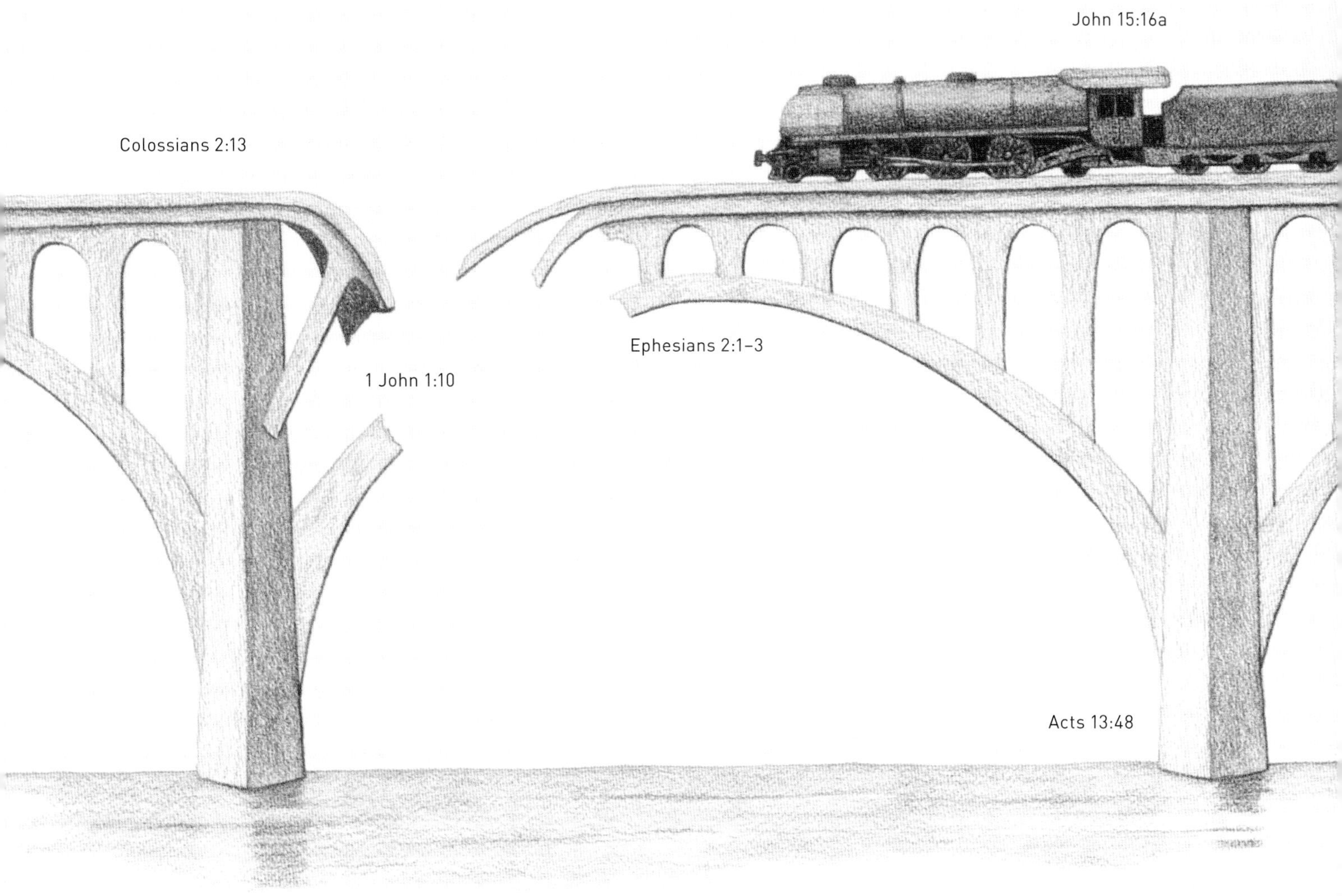

Colossians 2:13

1 John 1:10

Ephesians 2:1–3

John 15:16a

Acts 13:48

1 Corinthians 1:9

Romans 1:6

2 Thessalonians 2:13–14

40. Called

Magnets attract objects containing iron and hold onto them with an invisible power. If you place a metal object close to a magnet, you can feel the force of the magnet pulling it.

God's power to save his children and bring them into his family is like a spiritual magnet. No one can resist God's call. If your mom calls you to come back in the house from playing outside, you might decide to ignore her call and keep on playing; but when God calls his children, they always come.

Magnets have a limit to their power; that's why you can remove a metal object, like a paper clip, from off the magnet. But God's power has no limits and once God calls you to himself, you are his forever. Have you ever felt God calling you?

"No one can come to me unless the Father who sent me draws him."

JOHN 6:44a

But you are a chosen race, a royal priesthood, a holy nation, a people for his own possession, that you may proclaim the excellencies of him who called you out of darkness into his marvelous light.

1 PETER 2:9

God made the sun, moon, stars, and sky to show us how amazing he is. The moon and the stars, shining in the night sky, tell everyone about God's amazing power. God made sure that no one can say they didn't have a chance to believe. Even so, because sin makes us blind, people don't want to believe in God. But when God opens our eyes and calls us by name, we go to him—his call is irresistible.

If a million blind people had their sight restored, not one would want to keep their eyes shut for the rest of their life to stay blind and say No to seeing. It's the same with God's call. As he opens our eyes to see him, no one can resist the invitation to see him, know him, and live for him.

"I am sending you to open their eyes, so that they may turn from darkness to light and from the power of Satan to God, that they may receive forgiveness of sins and a place among those who are sanctified by faith in me."

ACTS 26:17b–18

Isaiah 43:1

1 Peter 5:10

1 Thessalonians 2:12

Acts 2:39

2 Corinthians 5:17

Ephesians 2:5

Ezekiel 36:26

John 3:1–3

Ephesians 2:1–2

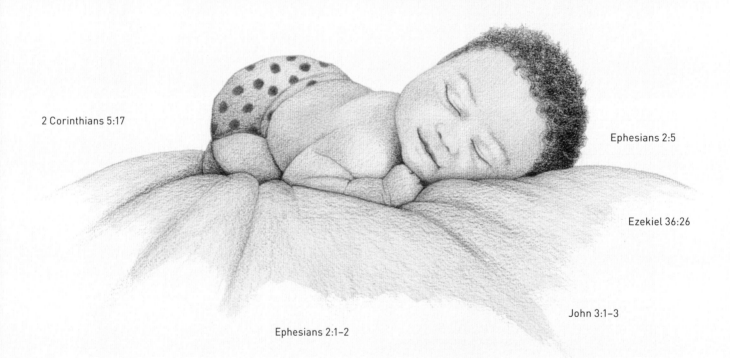

41. Born Again

Did you know that when God opens our eyes to see and believe in him, he also changes our heart from a hard stone that doesn't even want to get to know God to soft flesh that loves God? Then he calls us a brand new creation. When a baby is born, it takes its first breath and begins its journey through life. When we become a Christian, the Holy Spirit breathes new life into our spirit and makes us alive inside so that we can believe and begin a whole new journey of living for God. Jesus said that was like being born again!

A man named Nicodemus wanted to learn more about Jesus. When he went to him at night, Jesus told him this very important message: Unless a person is born again, he cannot see the kingdom of God. Being born again does not mean that someone comes out of his mother's body again; it means that someone who is dead in their sin is brought to life by the power of the Holy Spirit.

"Do not marvel that I said to you, 'You must be born again.' The wind blows where it wishes, and you hear its sound, but you do not know where it comes from or where it goes. So it is with everyone who is born of the Spirit."

JOHN 3:7–8

42. Faith

A delicious root beer float has only two main ingredients, root beer and vanilla ice cream. These two ingredients combine to form an amazing dessert.

Did you know that faith in Jesus has two ingredients? To become a Christian you need to believe, which means trusting that Jesus is God, died for your sins, and was raised from the dead. And you need to repent, which means you need to turn away from your sin and from going your own way and follow Jesus. This is what the Bible means by faith—believing and turning. Of course, even faith is a gift from God. We don't do anything to earn faith. The first time you turn to Jesus in faith, you become part of God's family. From then on, we have the Holy Spirit so we can keep believing and repenting whenever we sin. That's what it means to follow Jesus. Have you turned toward Jesus and asked him for forgiveness?

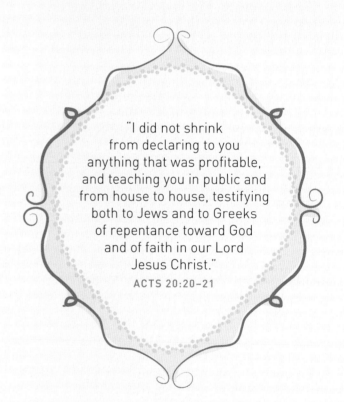

"I did not shrink from declaring to you anything that was profitable, and teaching you in public and from house to house, testifying both to Jews and to Greeks of repentance toward God and of faith in our Lord Jesus Christ."

ACTS 20:20–21

2 Chronicles 7:14

Acts 17:30

Hebrews 6:1

Acts 2:38

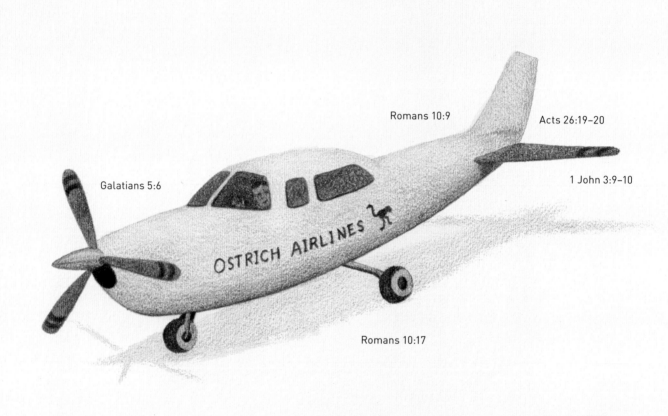

Galatians 5:6

Romans 10:9

Acts 26:19–20

1 John 3:9–10

OSTRICH AIRLINES

Romans 10:17

Airplanes need two important things to fly: wings to lift them and engines for power to push them through the air. If you have wings but no engine, your plane can't move. If you have an engine but no wings, you may speed up and down the runway but you will never take off. You need both to fly.

Putting your faith in Jesus always means growing in love for God and the people around you (Galatians 5:6). That's what Jesus meant when he said to obey his commands. If you think you are trusting in Jesus, but you don't love people, you are like an airplane with no wings. Jesus was clear that loving him means we must love others. On the other hand, sometimes people think they can live good lives without believing in Jesus. They trust in their own good works to save them. They are like airplanes with no engines. They can't even get off the ground. But Jesus said that faith in him was the only way to God. True Christians express their faith in love. You can't have one without the other. But don't forget that when you fail, you can turn to Jesus. He will always forgive you when you ask.

"If you love me, you will keep my commandments."
JOHN 14:15

"A new commandment I give to you, that you love one another: just as I have loved you, you also are to love one another."
JOHN 13:34

43. Jesus Paid It All

When you borrow money to buy something, you owe what we call a debt. Debts can be small, like if you borrow five dollars from your brother to buy a treat, or large, like when your parents borrow money from the bank to buy a house.

Making a mistake can also mean owing a debt. Imagine riding a wagon down a steep hill and then crashing through a neighbor's fence. Guess who has to pay for the fence? That's right, you do. If the price to replace the fence is three hundred dollars, you are instantly three hundred dollars in debt.

Much like destroying the picket fence, when Adam disobeyed God, he ruined the perfect, sinless life God gave him. But he didn't owe God just some money to fix a fence. He owed God a perfect life. That debt was impossible for him to pay. Jesus loved God and people perfectly. He didn't ruin his life or owe God a debt. Therefore, Jesus could pay Adam's and our debt to God with his perfect life.

God made [you]
alive together with him,
having forgiven us all our
trespasses, by canceling the
record of debt that stood against
us with its legal demands.
This he set aside, nailing
it to the cross.
COLOSSIANS 2:13b–14

Galatians 2:16

John 5:24

Galatians 5:4

Romans 3:20

Romans 5:9

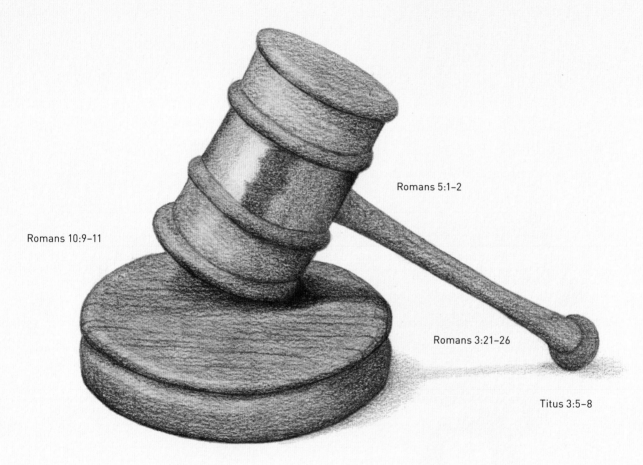

Romans 10:9–11

Romans 5:1–2

Romans 3:21–26

Titus 3:5–8

Romans 5:18

Imagine breaking a neighbor's fence, not having the money to repair it, and having to stand before a judge, knowing that you could spend a year in jail and still not come up with the money. But then, amazingly, your dad walks into the courtroom with a brand new section of fence as payment for your debt. Once he pays your debt, you are set free.

We all stand guilty like Adam before God, but instead of letting us die to pay our own debt, God sent Jesus to live a perfect life in our place and take our punishment on the cross, to pay our debt. Anyone who trusts Jesus is declared not guilty by God. There is a word to describe God's decision—justification. Those for whom Jesus died are justified—God the Father accepts Christ's sacrifice on the cross as payment for their debt of sin.

It will be counted to us who believe in him who raised from the dead Jesus our Lord, who was delivered up for our trespasses and raised for our justification.

ROMANS 4:24-25

44. Adopted

Imagine what it might be like for an orphan with no mother or father or brothers or sisters to be adopted into a large family. Think of the day when her new dad sweeps her up into his arms and gives her a big hug that says, "I'm never going to leave you or let you go, and I'm never going to let anyone take you away from me."

The next day the new daughter is introduced to the rest of her new family. There are three other children, all adopted like her, ready to welcome her with smiles, hugs, and laughter. What a difference it makes to be a part of a family!

The moment a person believes in Jesus, God adopts them into his big family. This is why Christians are called God's children. It is also why we call God "our Father" when we pray, and why we call other Christians our brothers and sisters.

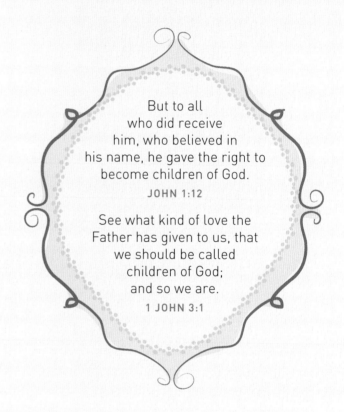

But to all who did receive him, who believed in his name, he gave the right to become children of God.
JOHN 1:12

See what kind of love the Father has given to us, that we should be called children of God; and so we are.
1 JOHN 3:1

Matthew 6:9

Galatians 3:23–26

2 Corinthians 6:16–18

Hebrews 12:6–11

1 Peter 1:3–7

Ephesians 5:1

Matthew 6:26–29

When you are adopted into a family, you get treated just like the children that were born into that family. And whatever the other children inherit from their parents, so you would inherit too. So when we are adopted into God's family, we are treated just like God the Father treats Jesus. Jesus becomes our brother and we share his inheritance with him! Not only that, God gives us the power to become like Jesus and grow to love him and other people. Instead of always thinking about ourselves and trying to get our own way, God changes us into his own dear sons and daughters who love him with our whole hearts. One day, when Jesus returns, we will even get new perfect bodies that will never get old or die.

Until that day, God, who is now our loving Father, is always with us. He uses everything, even the hard and sad things in life to make us more like Jesus. He doesn't always give us what we want because he knows what is best for us. Our faith is like gold, which has to be heated in a furnace to be made pure. Our faith is heated in the furnace of this life, by the hard things we face, to make it pure like gold.

Our troubles remind us to call on God for help. Just as God provides food for the birds and dresses the flowers in beautiful colors, so he will supply everything we need each day.

You have received the Spirit of adoption as sons, by whom we cry, "Abba! Father!" The Spirit himself bears witness with our spirit that we are children of God, and if children, then heirs—heirs of God and fellow heirs with Christ.

ROMANS 8:15b–17

The Ology
of Change

Romans 8:15

Galatians 5:1

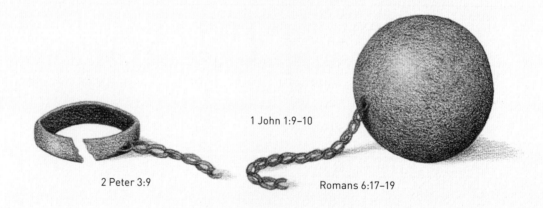

2 Peter 3:9

1 John 1:9–10

Romans 6:17–19

45. Sin Isn't in Charge Anymore

From the day Adam and Eve gave in to Satan's temptation and disobeyed God, sin was in charge of their lives. All of their children, including us, are just like them. We can't stop sinning even if we would want to. Just like a slave isn't free to make his or her own choices, we aren't free to follow God while sin is in charge. No one can escape sin and the death that comes with it.

But God sent his Son, Jesus, to break the power of sin. Jesus wasn't a slave to sin. Instead he loved God and others perfectly. Jesus didn't have to die for his own sins, so his death paid for the punishment we deserved.

Now, for those who trust in Jesus, sin isn't in charge anymore, but sin isn't completely destroyed yet either. You've probably already noticed how hard it is to stop wanting your own way and go God's way! But one day Jesus will return to end sin and death forever. The whole world will be free! Until that day, those who trust in Jesus are called to turn from sin and live for Jesus. When we ask for God's Spirit to live in us, we are given the power to say no to sin and yes to loving God and others. And when we fail, we know we can turn to Jesus for forgiveness and help. He is always right there beside us, forgiving and helping us.

We know that our old self was crucified with him in order that the body of sin might be brought to nothing, so that we would no longer be enslaved to sin. For one who has died has been set free from sin.

ROMANS 6:6–7

So you are no longer a slave, but a son, and if a son, then an heir through God.

GALATIANS 4:7

46. Set Apart, Holy for God

There is a difference between everyday dishes and fine china, which we only use for special times like holidays, anniversaries, and fancy dinners. China is often set apart in a cabinet behind glass doors where everybody can see it, while everyday dishes are stacked where no one can see them.

When God called us from darkness into his light and adopted us into his family, he set us apart like fine china to reflect his image in our lives. He sanctified us, which means he set us apart for his special use. When we are born again and join God's family, we are sanctified—set apart as holy for God. But while we have God's Spirit in us working to make us like Jesus, we often still want our own way instead of God's. Even though sin isn't in charge anymore, our struggle with sin continues. So every day we have to believe in Jesus and turn from our sin to live like the children of God we are. As we turn to God, the Holy Spirit opens our eyes, brings us from darkness to light, and makes us into a beautiful display that shows the whole world what Jesus looks and acts like.

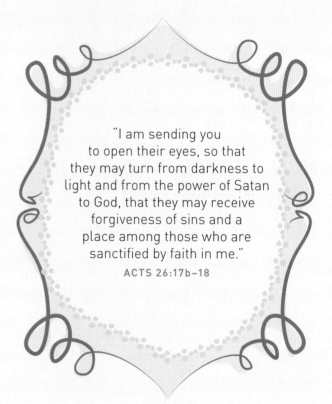

"I am sending you to open their eyes, so that they may turn from darkness to light and from the power of Satan to God, that they may receive forgiveness of sins and a place among those who are sanctified by faith in me."

ACTS 26:17b–18

2 Thessalonians 2:13

Ephesians 1:4

Acts 20:32

1 Corinthians 6:11

1 Peter 1:1–2

2 Corinthians 3:18

Ephesians 5:25–27

1 Thessalonians 4:3–4

47. We Grow a Little at a Time

God has set us apart, and is making us beautiful, but we all still struggle with wanting our way instead of God's way—in other words, we still sin! In our struggle, however, God is always at work making us more and more like Jesus.

Think of a person just learning how to ice skate. No matter how hard they try, they are going to take some falls. But as time goes on they make progress and learn how to skate longer and longer without falling. Even a professional figure skater hits the ice now and then. When they do, they pick themselves back up again and keep on skating. The better a skater gets, the more they see their need to grow and improve.

Living to reflect the image of God is a little bit like skating. Some days you do great, and other days you fall back into sin, but when you do fall, it is important to remember that Jesus died on the cross for that sin too, and to ask Jesus for forgiveness and then trust him again to help you become like him. The more we learn about Jesus the more we see just how much we need his help if we are going to think, talk, and act like him. We can only grow like Jesus as we depend on him for help every day. That's why Jesus said to ask for his Spirit every day.

Though the righteous fall seven times, they rise again.
PROVERBS 24:16 NIV

48. Put off the Old, Put on the New

No matter how comfortable your old shoes are, there is only one way to enjoy walking in a brand new pair of shoes. You've got to take off the old ones and put on the new ones. There is no way new shoes can be worn over old ones.

Our new life in Christ is like that. The Bible tells us that we have to put off our old self and put on the new self. The old self is our old way of living where we just think about ourselves and sin is in charge of us. Our new self is made to live as a free son or daughter of God. After God makes us all new—born again—isn't it silly to cling to our old sinful ways of living? Those old ways of living haven't done anything for us except make our lives miserable and sad. So we need to put off lying, meanness, anger, jealousy, and all the other sins that belong to our old way of life, and we need to put on Jesus, which means being kind, patient, and forgiving just like him. And the best part is, God gives us his Holy Spirit to help us. All we have to do is ask!

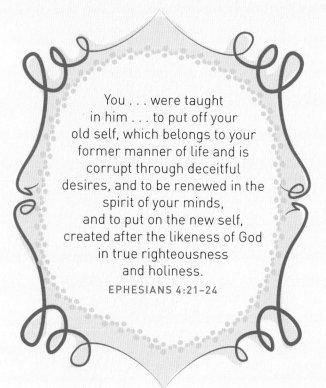

You . . . were taught in him . . . to put off your old self, which belongs to your former manner of life and is corrupt through deceitful desires, and to be renewed in the spirit of your minds, and to put on the new self, created after the likeness of God in true righteousness and holiness.

EPHESIANS 4:21–24

Colossians 3:9–14

Galatians 5:16

Romans 6:6; 13:14

Ephesians 4:25–29

Romans 8:26

John 14:26

John 16:13

Romans 7:21–23

49. The Holy Spirit Helps Us Fight Against Sin

The Bible describes our struggle with sin as a battle. Whenever we want to do good, evil is right there tempting us to do the wrong thing. Too often the good things we want to do, we do not do, and the bad things we do not want to do, we keep on doing. This battle continues throughout our lives and doesn't end until we go to be with Jesus in heaven. Until then the Holy Spirit helps us fight.

Just as Satan is always ready to tempt us to sin, the Holy Spirit is always ready to help us fight sin. He reminds us that going our own way will end up a big mess. He helps us to remember Bible verses, to pray, and to ask others to pray to keep us in step with God. And when we sin and the devil tries to make us feel like giving up or turning away from God, the Holy Spirit reminds us that we are God's sons and daughters, forgiven and loved. He reminds us that we cannot be separated from the love of God and that when we are weak God is strong.

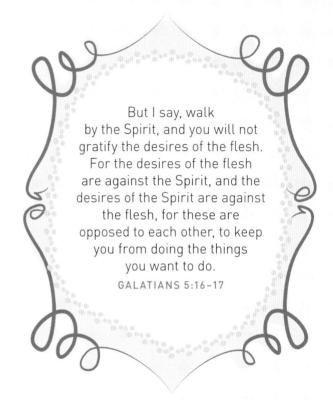

But I say, walk by the Spirit, and you will not gratify the desires of the flesh. For the desires of the flesh are against the Spirit, and the desires of the Spirit are against the flesh, for these are opposed to each other, to keep you from doing the things you want to do.

GALATIANS 5:16–17

50. The Fruit of the Spirit

The Bible compares the things that we say and do to fruit. The good things that we do are the good fruit, and the sinful things we do are the bad fruit. So what we say and do shows what kind of person we are.

When you see apples growing on a tree, you know it's an apple tree. You can also tell a good tree from a bad one by its fruit. If a tree is sick, the fruit is bad to eat; if the tree is healthy, the fruit is good to eat. In the same way, when we walk in step with the Spirit he makes us good on the inside. So then God's fruit grows in us—his love, joy, peace, patience, kindness, goodness, gentleness, and self-control. But when we are going our own way and giving into sin, we grow bad things like anger, jealousy, and fighting. You know a tree can't change the kind of fruit it grows or heal itself. But we have the Holy Spirit. Because we still have the disease of sin, sometimes we will grow bad fruit, but the Spirit of God can change us from the inside out! As we ask the Spirit to make us like Jesus, we will notice more and more good things growing in us. Have you noticed any good fruit lately in your life?

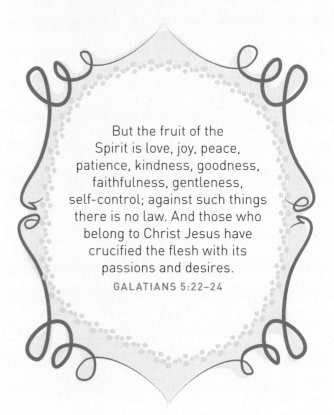

But the fruit of the Spirit is love, joy, peace, patience, kindness, goodness, faithfulness, gentleness, self-control; against such things there is no law. And those who belong to Christ Jesus have crucified the flesh with its passions and desires.

GALATIANS 5:22–24

Hebrews 12:11

Colossians 1:10

Galatians 5:18–24

Romans 7:4–5

Luke 6:43–45

John 10:28

James 1:12

Romans 5:2–5

1 Corinthians 9:24

Colossians 1:11–12

51. Running the Race to the End

Christianity is like a race, but it is not a sprint where you run as fast as you can for a short distance. It is a lifelong marathon that you run at your own pace. Everybody who crosses the finish line wins. In fact, the only way you can lose the race is to give up and stop running.

Like every race, we need to keep in mind the finish line and the prize we will get at the end. The prize in our race is Jesus. We finish the race at the end of our lives when we go to heaven to be with him. Life is the race, death is the finish line, and heaven with Jesus is our victory celebration.

When the going gets difficult and we get tired, it is okay to walk to catch your breath and regain your strength. Remember that Jesus, through his Spirit, is holding you, helping you, and walking with you. And God makes this promise: nobody, however weak or slow, whom he calls to run this race will ever be lost.

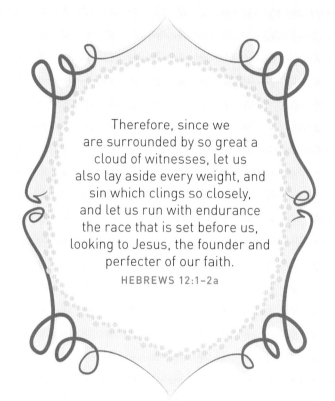

Therefore, since we are surrounded by so great a cloud of witnesses, let us also lay aside every weight, and sin which clings so closely, and let us run with endurance the race that is set before us, looking to Jesus, the founder and perfecter of our faith.

HEBREWS 12:1–2a

The Ology
of the
Church

Ephesians 2:22

1 Peter 2:5–6

1 Corinthians 6:19–20

52. The Church Is Built with Living Stones

When you hear the word *church*, what comes to mind? A big stone cathedral with stained glass windows? A small, white building with a pointed steeple?

The Bible does compare the church to a building, but its walls are made of living stones. The stones are the people who have believed and placed their faith in Christ. Jesus himself is the cornerstone, the first stone a builder lays in place. All the other stones in the building are lined up with the cornerstone to make sure they are set straight and true. In the same way, all believers are joined to Christ our Cornerstone and follow his Word to keep us straight and true. All together we form the living church of God.

While any place that people meet to worship God can be called a church, the true church is not the building; it's the believers inside. So when someone says they are going to church, don't think building, think people.

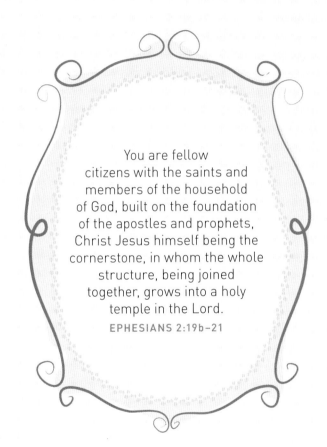

You are fellow citizens with the saints and members of the household of God, built on the foundation of the apostles and prophets, Christ Jesus himself being the cornerstone, in whom the whole structure, being joined together, grows into a holy temple in the Lord.
EPHESIANS 2:19b–21

53. The Church Is God's Temple

God's church, built with living stones, is also called a temple, the place where God's presence lives. Unlike the temple in Solomon's day, God's new temple is made of his people. That's because the Holy Spirit of God lives inside each of his children. That is why every believer is called the temple of the Holy Spirit and why Christians all together, as living stones, form the temple of God.

How wrong it is to throw rocks at a church's beautiful stained glass windows! As God's temple, our bodies are way more beautiful to God. When we sin, it is like throwing rocks at those windows.

The Bible also describes the church as a body with Jesus as the head. Just as different parts of the body have different jobs—legs do the running and eyes do the seeing—so the people who make up the church have different gifts and talents. Some people are gifted by God to lead while others are gifted to teach, care, or serve in other ways. One person's job is not better than another person's job, and the church needs everyone's gifts so it can work the way God intended.

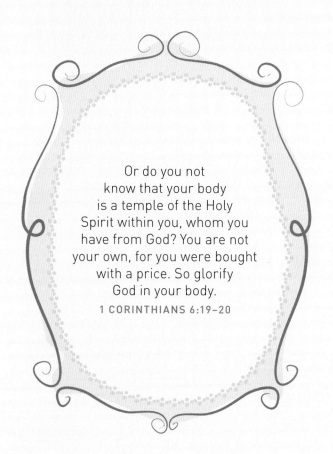

Or do you not know that your body is a temple of the Holy Spirit within you, whom you have from God? You are not your own, for you were bought with a price. So glorify God in your body.

1 CORINTHIANS 6:19–20

1 Corinthians 3:16–17

Colossians 1:17–20

Ephesians 1:22–23

Romans 12:4–5

1 Corinthians 12:14–18

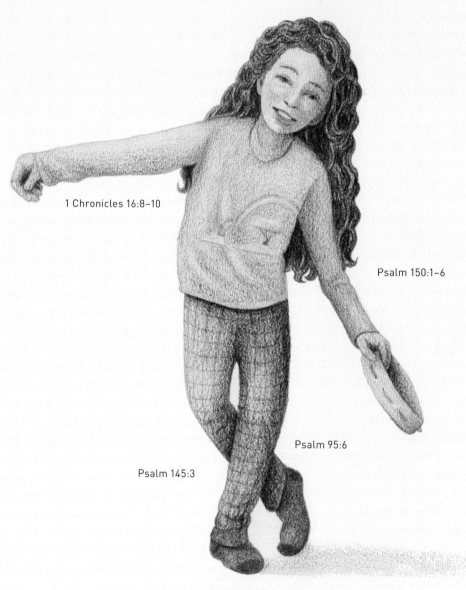

1 Chronicles 16:8–10

Psalm 150:1–6

Psalm 95:6

Psalm 145:3

John 4:21–24

54. We Gather to Worship

When we go to a sporting event and our team scores, we stand up and cheer for our team. When we gather for church on Sunday, we celebrate and worship Jesus and all he has done for us.

We can worship God by singing with a band or by praying quietly. We also worship by listening carefully to the message to see how God's Word applies to us. Did you know that it is even worship to meet with friends to talk about God and what he is doing?

We don't have to be in a church building to worship. We can read God's Word and pray or sing his praises anywhere. As the people of God we can worship him in everything we do if we do it all for his glory. So jump and run for God who gave you strong legs. Thank him for a sunny day, your family, your friends, every meal, and every blessing.

When you come together,
each one has a hymn,
a lesson, a revelation, a tongue,
or an interpretation. Let all
things be done for building up.
1 CORINTHIANS 14:26

Musical instruments are made to play music.
Nothing brings the violinmaker more joy than
the day when the construction of the body
is complete and he can make the wood sing.
Carefully he tunes the strings and rosins the bow.
Then with one wonderful stroke he draws the
bow across the strings and fills the room with
music. Violins were not made to sit on a shelf or
decorate a wall; they were made for one purpose,
to make beautiful music.

In the same way, we are made for one purpose, to
worship God—to give him all the glory. Nothing
brings God more joy than when we rejoice in
him above everything else.

So, whether you
eat or drink,
or whatever you do,
do all to the glory of God.
1 CORINTHIANS 10:31

Luke 4:8

Isaiah 12:5

Isaiah 43:6–7

Psalm 29:2

Hebrews 12:28

John 6:53–57

Matthew 26:26–29

Luke 22:19

1 Corinthians 11:23–32

55. The Lord's Supper

We take pictures of special events like birthday parties, vacations, and graduations to help us remember them. Later, we look at the pictures, which bring back memories of the fun things we've done.

While there were no cameras to take photos in Jesus's day, he did give us something special to remember him by. During the Last Supper, Jesus broke bread and gave it to his disciples and said, "'This is my body, which is for you. Do this in remembrance of me.' In the same way also he took the cup . . . saying, 'This cup is the new covenant in my blood. Do this, as often as you drink it, in remembrance of me'" (1 Corinthians 11:24–25).

Today, churches all around the world still remember Jesus and his death on the cross by celebrating the Lord's Supper. The breaking of the bread reminds us that the body of Jesus was broken, and the pouring of the cup reminds us that his blood was poured out for our sins. While the ordinary food we eat strengthens our body, eating the communion meal strengthens our souls as it reminds us of Jesus's sacrifice for us on the cross.

For as often as you eat this bread and drink the cup, you proclaim the Lord's death until he comes.

1 CORINTHIANS 11:26

56. Baptism

Before Jesus left the disciples he gave them this command: "Go out and make disciples of people from all nations, baptizing them in the name of the Father and of the Son and of the Holy Spirit." Ever since that day, when people believe in Jesus they are baptized with water. After the apostle Peter's first sermon at Pentecost, three thousand people believed and were baptized. New believers have been being baptized ever since.

In baptism, going under the water is a picture of how the person dies with Christ to their old sinful way of life. Coming out of the water is a picture of how, one day, we will rise from the dead, just as Jesus did.

Some Christian parents have their infant children baptized as a sign that they have been born into God's covenant family. Other parents wait until their children are old enough to turn away from their sin and say they believe in Jesus on their own before baptism. While not everyone agrees on the best time to baptize children of believers, wise leaders on both sides agree that all children must turn away from their sin and place their only hope for salvation in Jesus.

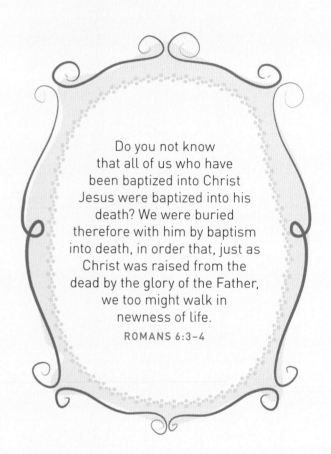

Do you not know that all of us who have been baptized into Christ Jesus were baptized into his death? We were buried therefore with him by baptism into death, in order that, just as Christ was raised from the dead by the glory of the Father, we too might walk in newness of life.

ROMANS 6:3–4

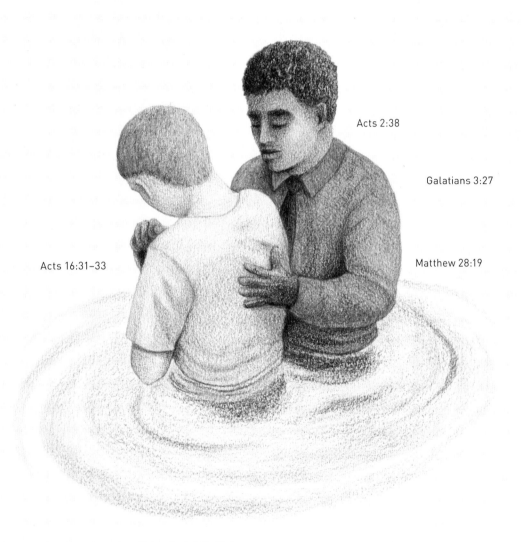

Acts 2:38

Galatians 3:27

Matthew 28:19

Acts 16:31–33

Colossians 2:11–12

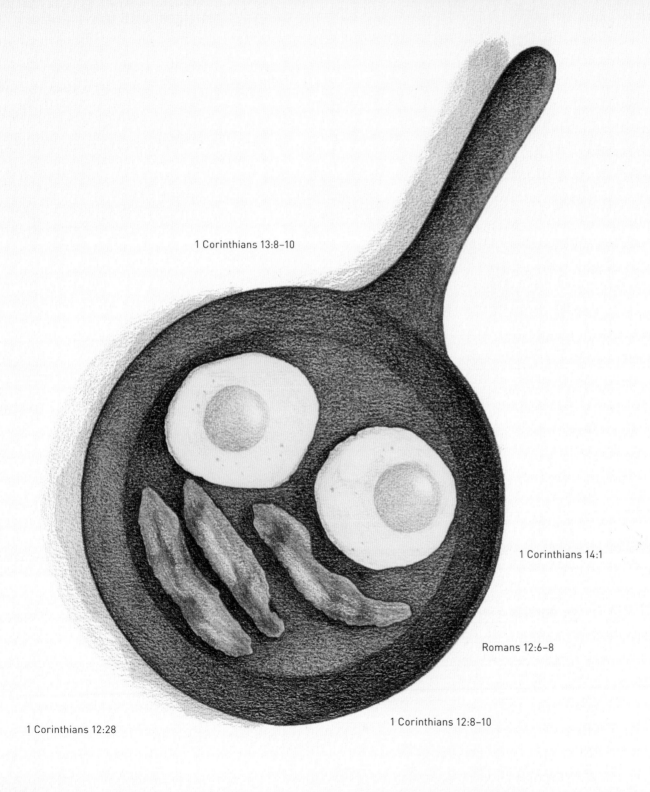

1 Corinthians 13:8–10

1 Corinthians 14:1

Romans 12:6–8

1 Corinthians 12:28

1 Corinthians 12:8–10

57. The Gifts of the Spirit

Children love to get gifts for their own enjoyment, for example, a jump rope or toy car. But did you ever notice that parents often receive gifts to help them serve others? The new frying pan or power screwdriver are not just for fun; they help the whole family. The frying pan will be used to make breakfast, and the power tool will be used to fix things that break around the house.

God gives the members of his church spiritual gifts to serve others in his family. Some of the gifts listed in the Bible include teaching, encouraging, leading, pastoring, healing, welcoming, and giving.

The Bible encourages us to ask for God's gifts so we can help the church and help others. But the greatest work of the Spirit is growing love in our lives. You may have many gifts, but if you don't use them in love, the church will not be blessed.

Now there are varieties of gifts, but the same Spirit; and there are varieties of service, but the same Lord; and there are varieties of activities, but it is the same God who empowers them all in everyone.

1 CORINTHIANS 12:4–6

58. Persecution of the Saints

Forest fires burn a terrible path of destruction when they strike. But it is the heat of those fires that opens the hardened cones of the lodge pole pine tree allowing them to spread their seeds. From those seeds, freshly planted, a new generation of saplings sprout, fed by the ashes of fallen trees. As strong winds scatter the fresh seed, the forest expands.

It didn't take long for the fires of persecution to attack the early church in Jerusalem. To escape arrest and even death, new Christians fled from the city. As they scattered, wherever they went they planted the seeds of the gospel, which God made grow. It is very sad that Christians were killed for believing in Jesus; however, their courage strengthened others and challenged them to live for Jesus. One book of the New Testament that was encouraging to Christians who suffered persecution was Revelation. In it the apostle John wrote about a vision from God, describing the victory of Jesus over all evil. Still today Revelation encourages believers to hold on to truth and keep going while they long for Christ's return.

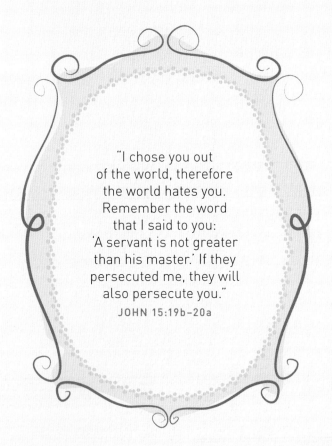

"I chose you out of the world, therefore the world hates you. Remember the word that I said to you: 'A servant is not greater than his master.' If they persecuted me, they will also persecute you."
JOHN 15:19b–20a

2 Corinthians 4:8–11

Acts 11:19

Matthew 5:11

Acts 8:1–4

The Ology
of the
End Times

2 Timothy 3:1

Zechariah 14:9

Revelation 22:6–7

Isaiah 42:9

2 Peter 3:3

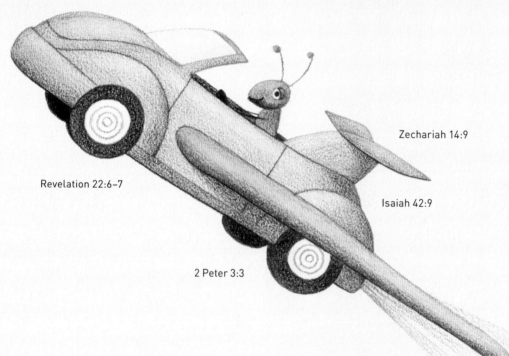

59. A Picture of the Future

Did you ever read a book that was so exciting that you couldn't resist peeking ahead at the last chapter? Some people think that's cheating, but others love to skip ahead to see how a story ends.

Nonfiction books tell of events that really happened in the past. Fiction books tell made-up stories, like an ant flying a car. Some authors write about what they imagine the future will be like, but they can only guess that there will be things like cars that fly or cities on distant planets.

There is one special book that does something amazing; it tells the future and because it was inspired by God who knows the future, it is absolutely true. The book, of course, is the Bible. The very last book, Revelation, describes God's judgment, the end of the world and the new heavens and earth. On the very last page Jesus gives us a special message to help make sure we are prepared for the end. He says, "I am coming soon."

"I am God, and there is no other; I am God, and there is none like me, declaring the end from the beginning and from ancient times things not yet done, saying, 'My counsel shall stand, and I will accomplish all my purpose.'"

ISAIAH 46:9b–10

60. The Return of Christ

When a king who is traveling through the countryside comes to a town, his arrival is announced by a fanfare played on brass instruments and by a herald who shouts out, "Here comes the King!" The greatest fanfare of all time and the greatest kingly introduction will come at the end of time when Jesus returns to earth.

People all over the world will be going about their daily chores or sleeping, when all at once the Lord Jesus will come down from heaven. The voice of the archangel will shout, announcing Christ's arrival, and trumpets will sound. No one will be able to sleep through his return.

Just as the flood came upon the people of Noah's day without warning, so will Christ's return to judge the earth catch many by surprise. The Bible tells us to be ready for Jesus to come back. You know for sure you are ready for Jesus's return when you put all your faith in him. Then when he comes back again, you will be welcomed into heaven as part of God's family.

While some people have tried to predict when Jesus will return, Jesus said that no one knows the day or hour, but only his Father in heaven.

But the day of the Lord will come like a thief, and then the heavens will pass away with a roar, and the heavenly bodies will be burned up and dissolved, and the earth and the works that are done on it will be exposed.

2 PETER 3:10

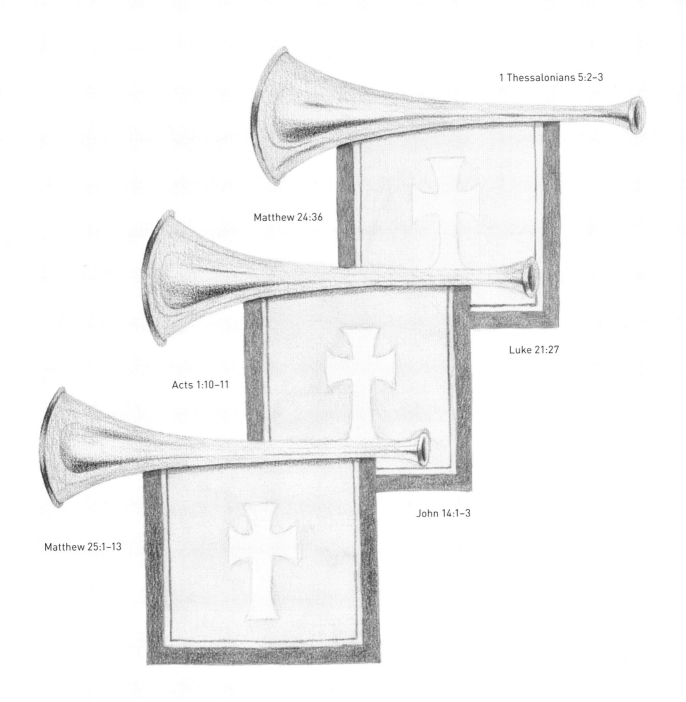

1 Thessalonians 5:2–3

Matthew 24:36

Luke 21:27

Acts 1:10–11

John 14:1–3

Matthew 25:1–13

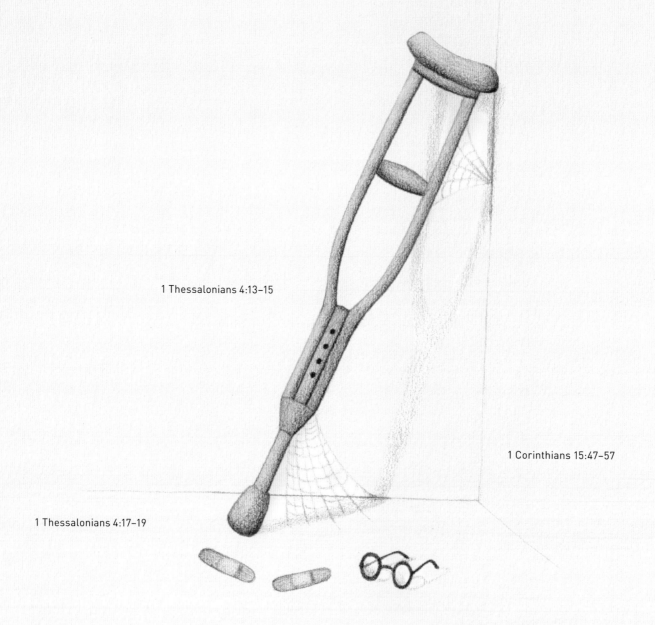

1 Thessalonians 4:13–15

1 Corinthians 15:47–57

1 Thessalonians 4:17–19

1 Corinthians 15:35–44

When Jesus, robed in glorious light, returns to the earth, he will shout a command and, amazingly, the bodies of everyone who died trusting in Jesus will rise again from the dead. Can you imagine thousands of people rising up from their graves all at once? Their spirits, which went to be with Jesus in heaven when they died, will rejoin their brand new, glorified bodies and rise to meet Jesus in the air. Like the resurrected body of Jesus, these new bodies will be completely free of sin, sickness, and death. Those who were crippled in life will rise with new legs; those who had cancer will be healed; those who were blind will see, the deaf will hear, and those who couldn't even speak will sing.

Then the believers who are still alive when Jesus returns will receive new bodies too. They will rise up into the sky and join all of God's family from the past. People we read about in the Bible will be there too. Sarah, Rachel, Mary, Elizabeth, Moses, Elijah, John the Baptist, and Paul will all be there that day, caught up with Jesus in the clouds.

For the Lord himself will descend from heaven with a cry of command, with the voice of an archangel, and with the sound of the trumpet of God. And the dead in Christ will rise first.

1 THESSALONIANS 4:16

61. The Final Judgment

After Christ returns and takes the believers with him, those who rejected Jesus will realize they've been wrong. People who said things like, "There is no God; the universe created itself," and those who didn't think they needed Jesus and said things like, "All roads lead to heaven," will not be changed. They will not get new glorified bodies. Instead, they will face judgment. When Christ takes his judgment throne, those left on earth will run in fear to hide behind rocks and in caves hoping the rocks themselves would crash upon them.

In the midst of that panic, all those who rejected Jesus will be called out of hell to face God's judgment. As the Bible prophesies, all those who did not believe while on earth, will now have no choice but to bow their knee and declare that Jesus Christ is Lord. They will then have to stand and be judged before God's throne.

For an hour is coming when all who are in the tombs will hear his voice and come out, those who have done good to the resurrection of life, and those who have done evil to the resurrection of judgment.

JOHN 5:28b–29

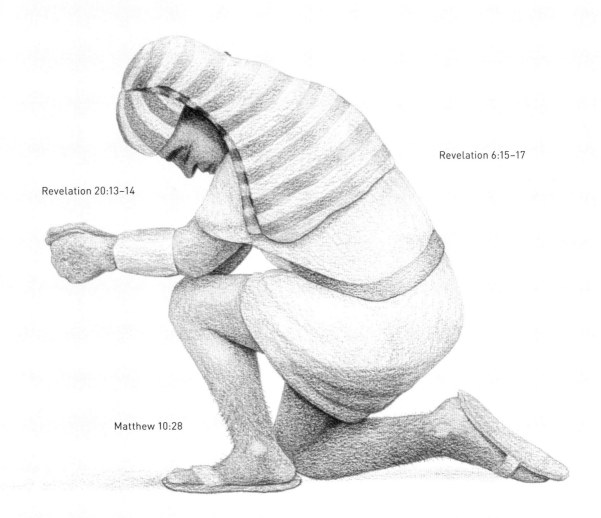

Revelation 6:15–17

Revelation 20:13–14

Matthew 10:28

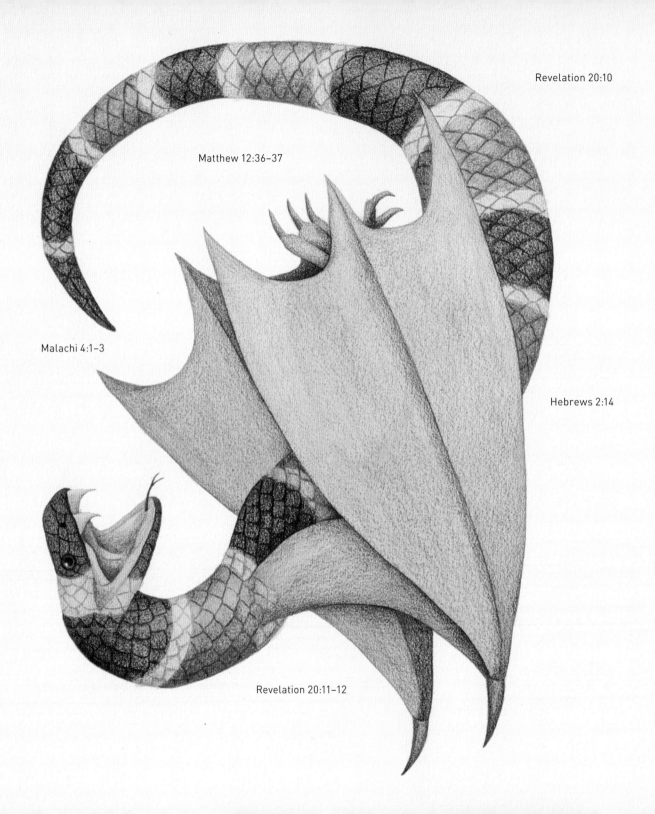

Revelation 20:10

Matthew 12:36–37

Malachi 4:1–3

Hebrews 2:14

Revelation 20:11–12

On that day, the record books of heaven will be opened and read. Every hidden sin will be shouted out for all to hear. Every murder, theft, lie, and even every unkind word or thought will be revealed, as each unbeliever is judged for their sins. Those whose names are not found in the Book of Life will be sent away from God forever. The Bible calls this place by many names—hell, the lake of fire, the second death—all of them stand for a place where there is no love and no life. Only in God can we find life and love.

Once and for all the great dragon himself, the devil, will be cast down forever where he will suffer day and night because of all the evil and mean things he has done. The heavens and the earth as we now know them will pass away. Like the earth during the flood of Noah's day, it will once again be scrubbed clean of all sin and evil. But this time there won't be any sin left to spoil the new, clean world. God will make the heavens and the earth brand new.

And he who was seated on the throne said, "Behold, I am making all things new." Also he said, "Write this down, for these words are trustworthy and true."

REVELATION 21:5

62. A Very Different Day for All God's Children

When you trust in Jesus, the last day of this earth will be very different for you. You too will stand before God, but instead of having to answer for all your sins, you can just point to Jesus and say, "I'm with him!" Jesus's death on the cross has already paid for all of your sins. So when you stand before God, you will be welcomed by these words, "Well done, good and faithful servant." How amazing is that? On that day we will really understand what it means to be forgiven and have our sin put as far away from God as the east is from the west.

Christ will give us crowns of everlasting life and perfect righteousness. Our struggle with doing and thinking bad things will be over. Our struggle with fear, sadness, and even death will be over! Instead of tears, we will be all singing and shouting, "Worthy are you, our Lord and God, to receive glory and honor and power." The very best thing about that day will be seeing God face-to-face and getting to worship him.

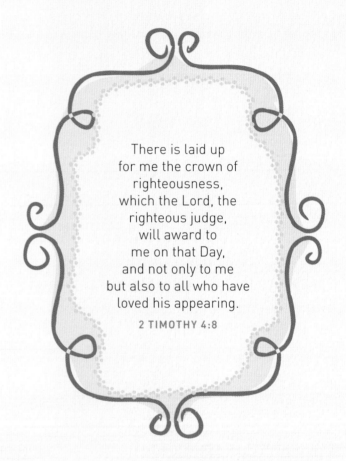

There is laid up for me the crown of righteousness, which the Lord, the righteous judge, will award to me on that Day, and not only to me but also to all who have loved his appearing.

2 TIMOTHY 4:8

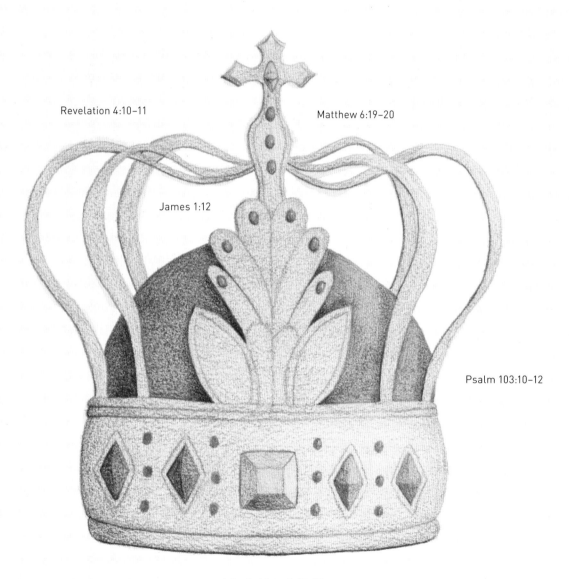

Revelation 4:10–11

Matthew 6:19–20

James 1:12

Psalm 103:10–12

1 Corinthians 3:12–15

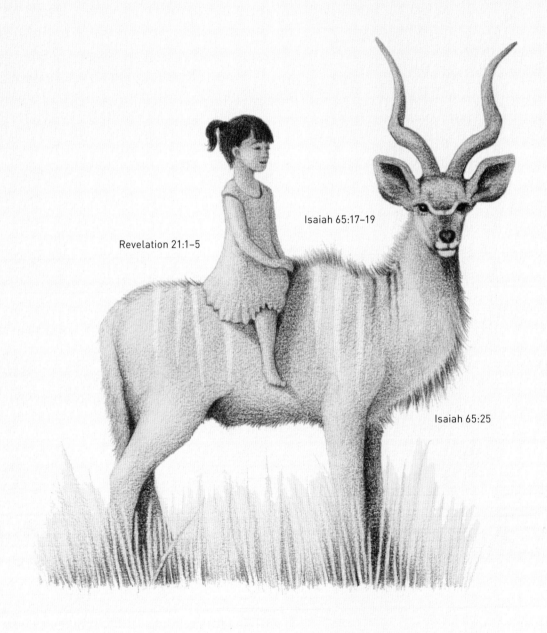

Revelation 21:1–5

Isaiah 65:17–19

Isaiah 65:25

63. The New Heavens and Earth

Have you ever been so happy to get back home and into your own bed after a long trip? That is just a small piece of what heaven will be like for God's children. While heaven can seem far away and hard to understand, when God makes the earth brand new again, we will have so much joy because we are finally home. That joy will fill our lives and bubble over in praise to God for all he has done.

We will watch as the New Jerusalem, the city God has prepared for us, descends from the sky to earth. Imagine what it will be like to walk through its crystal gates realizing that it will be our home forever! Within its beautiful walls we will live with Jesus, building homes, tending gardens, making music, creating art, and in all kinds of different ways filling the world with beauty and joy.

Animals will once again fill the earth and, like in the garden of Eden, they will live in peace and harmony together with us. Imagine petting a tiger, riding an antelope, or calling for an eagle to perch on your arm.

Then I saw a new heaven and a new earth, for the first heaven and the first earth had passed away, and the sea was no more. And I saw the holy city, new Jerusalem, coming down out of heaven from God, prepared as a bride adorned for her husband. And I heard a loud voice from the throne saying, "Behold, the dwelling place of God is with man."
REVELATION 21:1–3a

While the earth will be beautiful, nothing will compare to the center of the New Jerusalem. There Jesus will sit on his throne and welcome us in. The river of the water of life, bright as crystal, will flow from his throne through the streets. The tree of life will grow near the river unguarded, its fruit free for the taking.

The glorious light of Christ will radiate from his throne and light up the whole world. We will see Christ as he is and gaze at him face-to-face, unafraid and unblinded by his light and goodness.

Even the best things of earth will fade; nothing will compare with our love for Jesus. We will be completely happy just being with Jesus, and that will bring him the greatest joy.

They will see his face, and his name will be on their foreheads. And night will be no more. They will need no light of lamp or sun, for the Lord God will be their light, and they will reign forever and ever.

REVELATION 22:4–5

Revelation 22:1–3

Isaiah 60:19–20

1 Corinthians 13:12

1 Timothy 6:16

1 John 3:2

John 14:2–3

Revelation 21:17–27

Revelation 3:12

64. The Special Place Where God Lives with His People

Stadiums for sporting events can hold a lot of people. But imagine what it will be like when all the millions and millions of Christians from all time are gathered together in the New Jerusalem around the throne to worship.

The city called New Jerusalem pictured in the book of Revelation is described as being very, very large— immense even. John tells us in his book that the city is 12,000 stadia on each side. That is more than a thousand miles long! It would, in fact, cover most of the United States and be taller than two hundred fifty mountains stacked one on top of the other!

But the measurements mean more than just that the city will be enormous. The large size of the city is a picture of how big God's plan and purpose is for his people and the new heavens and earth. The city is also described as a cube—all the sides are equally long. In Solomon's temple in the Old Testament, the most holy place—the place that represented God's presence—was also a cube. But in the New Jerusalem that cube will be many, many, many times larger because God will not only be in the most holy place of the temple, he will fill the whole, immense space. The whole city will be the special place where God will live with his people.

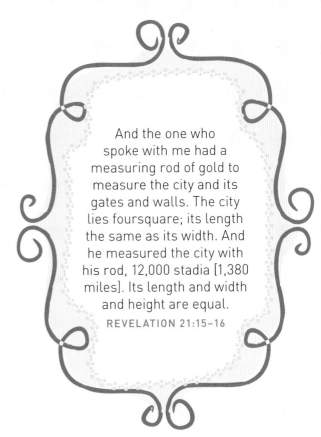

And the one who spoke with me had a measuring rod of gold to measure the city and its gates and walls. The city lies foursquare; its length the same as its width. And he measured the city with his rod, 12,000 stadia [1,380 miles]. Its length and width and height are equal.

REVELATION 21:15–16

In the center court of the enormous New Jerusalem, people from every nation, tribe, and language will gather. There will be so many people that no one will be able to count them all. (Just like God said, comparing them to the sands of the seashore and the stars of the sky!) Together they will worship God saying, "Salvation belongs to our God who sits on the throne, and to the Lamb." In addition to millions of believers, thousands and thousands of angels will join the celebration. They will shout, "Blessing and glory and wisdom and thanksgiving and honor and power and might be to our God forever and ever! Amen!"

On that day every promise of God will be fulfilled: the promise to Adam to crush the head of the serpent; the promise to Abraham to make his children as numerous as the sands of the sea; the promise to David that one of his offspring will reign on the throne forever, and the promise to us that if we put our faith in Jesus Christ we will be saved.

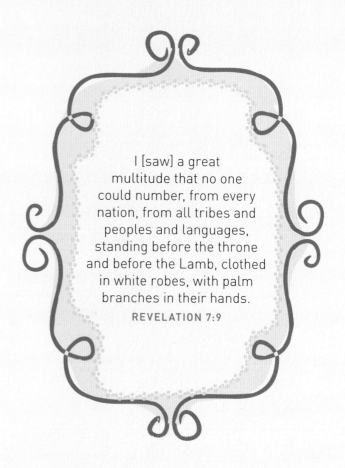

I [saw] a great multitude that no one could number, from every nation, from all tribes and peoples and languages, standing before the throne and before the Lamb, clothed in white robes, with palm branches in their hands.

REVELATION 7:9

Revelation 7:10–17

Revelation 22:16–21

Revelation 22:6–10

Genesis 22:17

Jeremiah 33:17–18

Ephesians 5:22–31

Matthew 25:13

Mark 2:19

John 3:25–30

John 14:3

65. The Final Wedding

From the day when God created Eve and brought her to Adam, their joining in marriage spoke a hidden message. The love of a husband for his bride reflects the love of Christ for his church. A man and a woman becoming one in marriage is a picture of the church, the people of God, and Jesus joining together in a heavenly marriage at the end of the age. All the wedding celebrations on earth point to that greater wedding day and the celebration we will have in the New Jerusalem.

Marriage shows the world the greatness of God's love for us. That is why husbands and wives are called to love and honor one another. God wants husbands and wives to show the world his unending love for the church and for the church to show their honor of Christ. At the end of the age, we will be joined to Jesus and live with him forever. Our marriage to Jesus will never end.

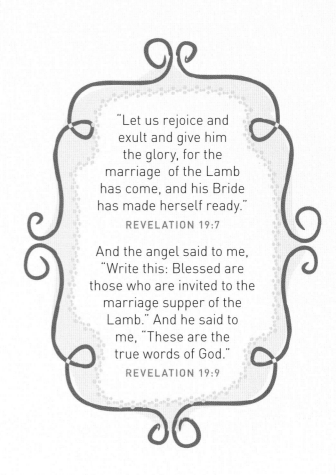

"Let us rejoice and exult and give him the glory, for the marriage of the Lamb has come, and his Bride has made herself ready."

REVELATION 19:7

And the angel said to me, "Write this: Blessed are those who are invited to the marriage supper of the Lamb." And he said to me, "These are the true words of God."

REVELATION 19:9

The Ology
of God's
Word

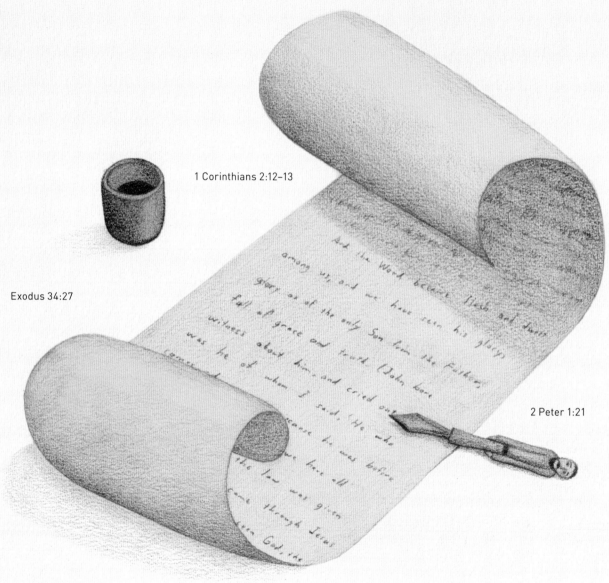

1 Corinthians 2:12–13

Exodus 34:27

2 Peter 1:21

Revelation 21:5

66. God Wrote the Bible Through People

The apostle Paul told Timothy that the Bible was "breathed out by God." That means that God was inspiring the writers of the books of the Bible to record the words of God. Paul told the Corinthians that the Spirit of God gave him the words he used to teach them God's truth.

When you use a pen to write a letter or a note, the pen puts the ink on the page and the ink forms the words. When the letter is complete, you could say the pen was the instrument for writing the letter. Yet if your hand did not move the pen, it could write nothing.

In a similar way, the writers of the Bible—with their own personalities and language—were like pens in the hand of God. God inspired them to remember what they saw and to write down what God wanted them to write. So while the Bible was written by people, God was the author behind it.

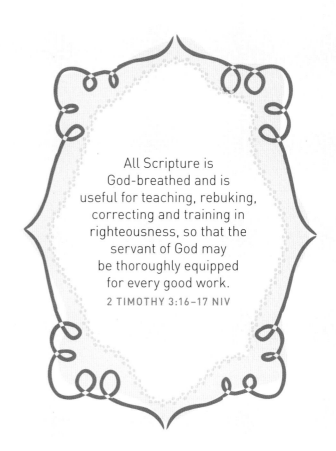

All Scripture is God-breathed and is useful for teaching, rebuking, correcting and training in righteousness, so that the servant of God may be thoroughly equipped for every good work.

2 TIMOTHY 3:16–17 NIV

67. God's Word Is True

A lie is saying something that is not true. People tell lies to stay out of trouble, like telling your mom you ate all your broccoli when you actually fed it to your dog. People also tell lies to trick others, like saying you caught a huge fish that was actually really small.

The Bible tells us that God is very different than us, for he can never lie. One of the names Jesus gave himself was the Truth. When God gave us his Word he gave us his truth. He made sure that the men who wrote it down, inspired by the Holy Spirit, did not make any mistakes and only told the truth. That is why we can trust the Bible to direct our lives.

Every word of
God proves true;
he is a shield to those
who take refuge in him.
PROVERBS 30:5

Sanctify them in
the truth; your word
is truth.
JOHN 17:17

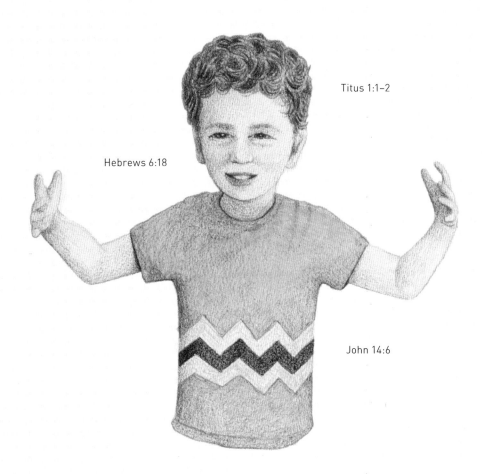

Hebrews 6:18

Titus 1:1–2

John 14:6

Romans 15:4

Revelation 22:18–19

Numbers 23:19

When writing a note, did you ever misspell a word? For example, suppose you leave a note for your mom that says, "Ples remember too wak me up for skool." What if your brother finds the note and reads "w-a-k" not as "wake," but as "whack," and thinks you want him to whack you when it's time to get up. Then when the time comes he starts whacking you with a pillow!

Over the years, scribes copied the Bible again and again so that people all over the world could read it. Even though the scribes were painstakingly careful, they sometimes made tiny mistakes. Scholars have tried to correct these mistakes, but even so, they cannot be sure that they've corrected them all. Regardless, the Bible is very close to the way it was originally written, and none of these tiny errors affect the truth of God's saving plan through Jesus's death on the cross.

Some have used the presence of copying mistakes as an excuse to say we can't trust the Bible. But when we compare the Bible of today with the earliest copies, it is clear that God has protected his Word so that none of his message has been lost.

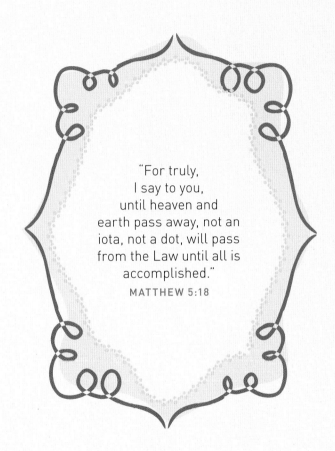

"For truly, I say to you, until heaven and earth pass away, not an iota, not a dot, will pass from the Law until all is accomplished."
MATTHEW 5:18

68. God Talks to You and You Talk to God

Think of your best friend. How did you get to know this friend? Most likely, you talked to her and she talked to you and gradually you came to know each other well. This is how it is with God. God talks to us through his Word, the Bible, and we talk to God by praying.

Of course, God already knows everything about us. But everything we need to know about God we can find out by reading his Word. What's more, the Holy Spirit uses the words in the Bible to speak to us. He shows us how much we need Jesus. He comforts us when we are sad. He reminds us that, because of Jesus's death, we can be forgiven for our sins and become God's dearly loved child. The Holy Spirit uses the Bible to teach us how to live for God.

God talks to us through his Word and, when we pray, we can talk to God just like we talk to a friend. God promises that he always hears us. We can tell God how much we love him and ask for his help. We can ask God to help others too. When Jesus lived on earth, his friends often saw him praying, and Jesus told them to pray too. Because they were not sure what to say to God, they asked Jesus to teach them to pray. We call the prayer that Jesus taught them the "Lord's Prayer" (see Matthew 6:9–13).

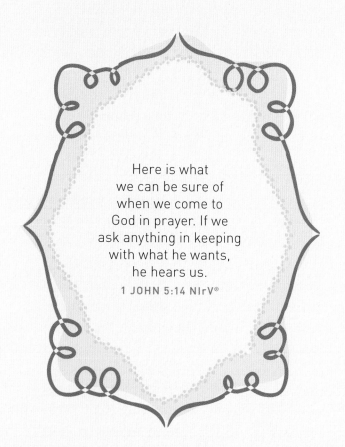

Here is what we can be sure of when we come to God in prayer. If we ask anything in keeping with what he wants, he hears us.

1 JOHN 5:14 NIrV®

1 Thessalonians 5:17

Psalm 62:8

Luke 11:1

Matthew 6:9–13

2 Timothy 3:16–17

Philippians 4:6

Jeremiah 15:16

Romans 10:13–17

Matthew 4:4

2 Timothy 2:15

69. The Bible Is Our Spiritual Food

When a fawn or other animal is orphaned and then rescued from the wild, one of the first things a veterinarian will do is give it something to eat. But if the fawn is afraid, it may not want to eat. In that case the vet might have to force it to eat because without food it can't survive.

God created us to feel hunger when we've missed a meal or two because, like animals, people need food to live and grow. But unlike animals, people also need spiritual food. We need to read God's Word so that we can continue to learn about God and learn more about how to live for him.

Just like you can fill up on candy and soda but not get the vitamins you need to grow, you can learn a lot of good things from the world around you but not have the important truth you need to live and grow with God. Only the Bible contains the words of life each person needs to know to be saved and grow as a Christian.

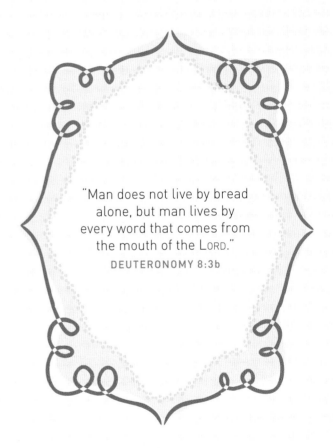

"Man does not live by bread alone, but man lives by every word that comes from the mouth of the Lord."
DEUTERONOMY 8:3b

70. The Holy Spirit Helps Us Understand God's Word

Diamond mine shafts can be more than a mile deep. You don't have to go very far into them before it is pitch black. That is why miners work with headlamps. In the dark, diamonds are like any other rock, but the headlamp helps the miner find the diamond crystal.

In much the same way, the Holy Spirit illuminates (helps us understand) God's Word so that we can see the treasure of truth it contains. Without the Holy Spirit, people are like miners fumbling around in the dark. They may read Jesus's words, "Come to me, all who are weary and I will give you rest," but not realize the Bible is speaking to them personally. It is the Holy Spirit who helps us to see and understand Jesus's invitation to come. As we read, the Holy Spirit helps us to understand how God's Word applies to us. Just as a diamond mine is deep, so the truth of God's Word runs deep. You could spend your whole life on mining God's Word and there would still be an eternity of discoveries to uncover.

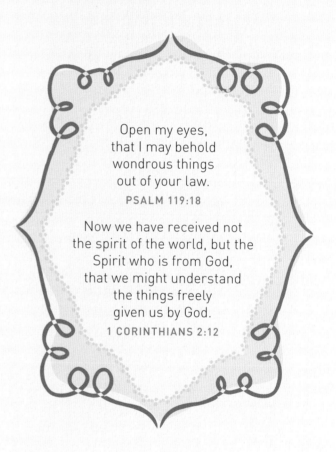

Open my eyes,
that I may behold
wondrous things
out of your law.
PSALM 119:18

Now we have received not
the spirit of the world, but the
Spirit who is from God,
that we might understand
the things freely
given us by God.
1 CORINTHIANS 2:12

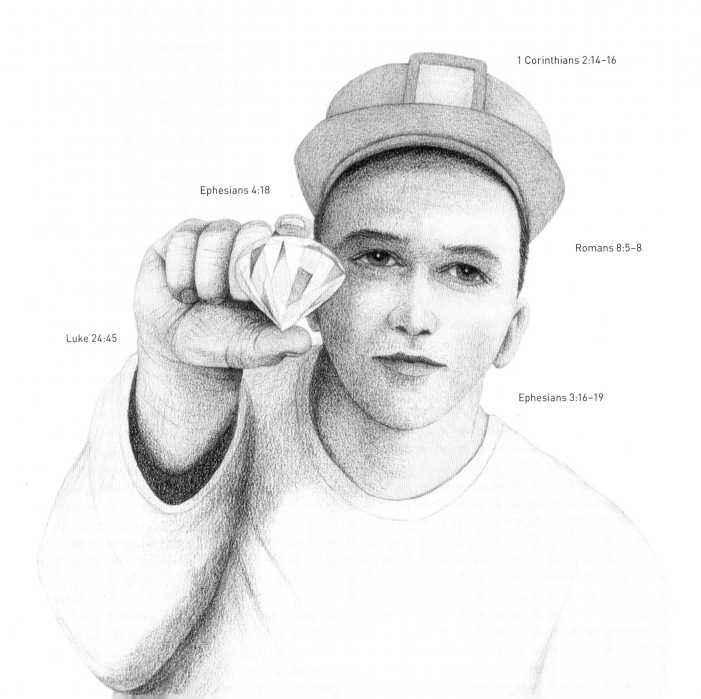

1 Corinthians 2:14–16

Ephesians 4:18

Romans 8:5–8

Luke 24:45

Ephesians 3:16–19

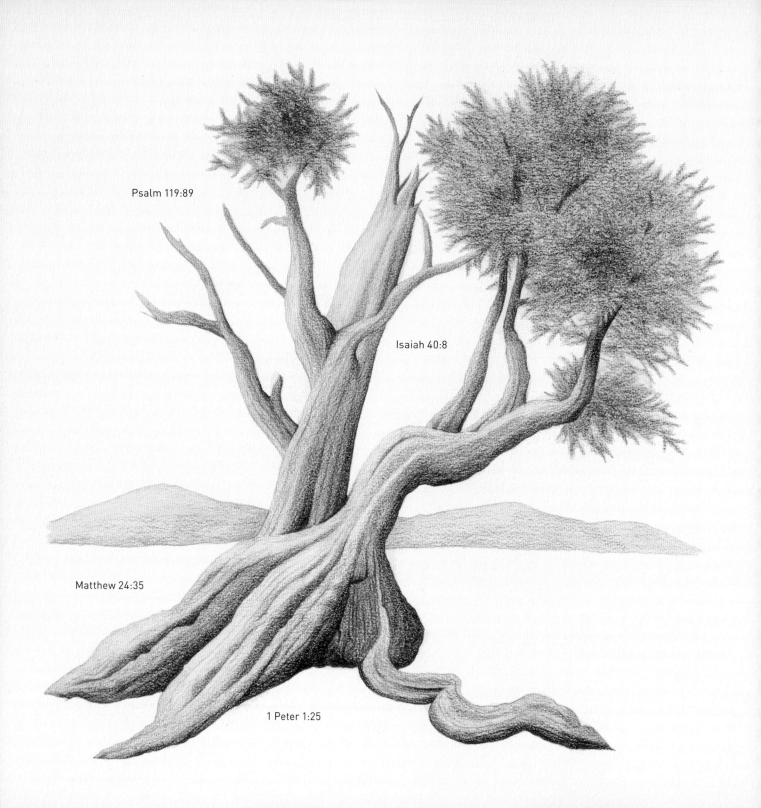

Psalm 119:89

Isaiah 40:8

Matthew 24:35

1 Peter 1:25

71. The Word of God Lives Forever

Bristlecone pine trees with their gnarled, bare branches are often mistaken for dead, yet some of them are over four thousand years old and still growing! One of the oldest known bristlecones has been nicknamed Methuselah after the man in the Bible who lived 969 years. Methuselah the tree is over 4,750 years old!

Some people view God's Word as just another dusty book of ancient history. The Bible, however, is very much alive, still speaking to every generation who opens it up and reads it. It is the only book whose message, the gospel of Jesus Christ, is able to bring people from spiritual death back to life.

While heaven and earth as we know them will one day pass away, God's Word will never pass away. God's Word is eternal and will last forever. So open the Bible and read it. As you study its pages, you'll meet Jesus, learn the words of life, and hear the call of God to turn from your sin and live for him.

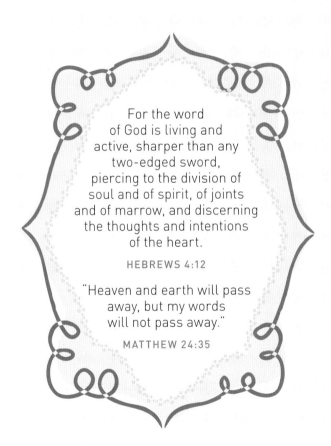

For the word of God is living and active, sharper than any two-edged sword, piercing to the division of soul and of spirit, of joints and of marrow, and discerning the thoughts and intentions of the heart.

HEBREWS 4:12

"Heaven and earth will pass away, but my words will not pass away."

MATTHEW 24:35

As they finished the last

page, a thought popped into Carla's mind. "It's not over," she said. "There's more!"

"What do you mean? We read the last page," Timothy replied with a confused look on his face.

Carla turned to a random page and pointed, "See the names and numbers in the pictures? These are verses from the Bible, and I'm sure that if we look them up, they will add to the story on the page where they're found."

"I get it," mused Timothy. "*The Ology* is only the beginning. It's meant to point us back to God's Word."

"Let's take it home and look at it again with our Bibles," Carla suggested.

"Great idea," Timothy agreed. "Let's go!"

Glossary

Important Bible Words You Should Know and Understand

Atone (atonement) *to cover*
How the blood of Jesus shed on the cross covers our sin and restores our relationship with God so that it is brand new.

Glory *perfect splendor*
The display of one or more of God's attributes—his holiness, perfection, love, mercy, and justice, to name a few. John says that Jesus glorified the Father by going to the cross (John 17:1–5). That's because Jesus dying for his people was the greatest display of love in the whole world. When we love people like Jesus did, we display God's glory too.

Gospel *good news*
Jesus's story including his sinless life, sacrificial death, and resurrection from the dead. It is the source of our forgiveness and eternal life and what the Holy Spirit uses to open our eyes to believe.

Grace *freely given*
Used to describe the free gift of eternal life God gives to all his children. Salvation is all grace, a free gift from God, just because he loves us. The greatest grace we receive is God himself!

Holy *exalted*
Used to describe God who is exalted above all else; he is completely different than we are. His thoughts are higher than our thoughts and he is perfect in everything he does. God is sometimes said to be "other"—completely awesome, amazing, and worthy of the highest praise.

Justify (justification) *to declare not guilty*
Used to describe God's "not guilty" decision over us. God declares us guilty sinners not guilty because Jesus paid the penalty for our sin. When you see the word *justified*, think "no longer guilty," and "Jesus paid it all."

Love, God's *selfless, sacrificial, unconditional love*
God's love encompasses sacrifice and commitment. Sacrifice means to give up something, exemplified when Jesus gave his life for us. Commitment means loving not because the loved person deserves it but because the person who loves decides to do so. Love isn't love if you take back what you gave. In marriage, for example, a husband and wife give their lives for one another and promise to be married until death parts them.

Mercy *compassion*

Used to describe getting something good instead of what is deserved. God shows us mercy when, because of Jesus's death on the cross for us, he spares us the punishment we deserve and forgives us instead.

Repent *to turn*

When we are sorry for sin, we repent—turn from our sins. We ask God for forgiveness for Jesus's sake and the power to live differently.

Righteousness (righteous) *right-ness*

Perfectly "right" in the eyes of God. The opposite is "wrong-ness," which is sin. Jesus lived a perfectly righteous life—he never sinned—and he trades his perfect life for our sin-filled one. That is how we can become righteous even though we are sinners.

Sacrifice *to give something up*

Used to describe the giving up of one life for another. In the Old Testament, animals died in place of the sinners who offered them; these sacrifices pointed to Jesus's atoning sacrifice.

Save (salvation) *rescue*

Jesus died in our place to rescue or save us from spiritual death—an eternity separated from God.

Sanctify (sanctified) *set apart*

Used to describe the way something is set apart for special use. For example, you set apart your best dress clothes for special occasions—you sanctify them. God saves his people, setting them apart for his special use—God sanctifies those he saves. When we sin, we repent and God forgives us for Jesus's sake. The Holy Spirit makes us grow to be more like Jesus. In this way, sanctification continues throughout our lives.

Sin *to miss the mark*

Like when an arrow flies wide of the target's bullseye, when we sin, we miss the mark of God's righteousness. Sin includes anything we think or do that is against or breaks God's law. God's laws are all about how to love God and people. So when we sin we are not being loving; we go our own way instead of God's way.

Wrath, God's *holy anger*

Used to describe God's response to sin. Holy anger backed up by God's almighty power to destroy all evil. Because of God's grace, mercy, and love, Jesus took God's wrath on himself. God's wrath for sin was poured out on Jesus, so now God's people do not get wrath, they get love.

Think Theology, Talk Theology

(Questions)

The Ology of God

1. God Always Was and Always Will Be
List all the names and characteristics for God mentioned in the Scripture verses in this chapter.

2. God Is Three in One
Which of the verses mentions all three persons of the Trinity together in one place?

Read John 14:26. How does it explain the Trinity?

3. God Created Everything out of Nothing at All
Who does Colossians 1:16 refer to?

What does the passage from Isaiah tell us we can learn about God from his work in creation?

4. God Is All-Powerful
What proclaims God's handiwork?

What verse tells us that people have no excuse for refusing to believe in God?

5. God Is in Control
What does God command to fall upon the earth?

What does every man and woman get from God?

6. God Knows All Things
Which verse tells us that God knows everything?

Rewrite Hebrews 4:13 in your own words. Describe how this verse makes you feel.

7. God Is Everywhere
Rewrite Psalm 139:7–10 in your own words.

8. God Is Perfect
Which verse(s) tells us what perfect love looks like?

Who do you find hard to love? What can you do to love them better?

The Ology of People

9. God Created Man and Woman in His Image
In whose likeness did God create man and woman? Which verse tells us that?

List some ways that men and women are different from animals?

10. The First Husband and Wife
How are men and women the same? How are they different?

What did Adam name the wife God created from his rib?

11. God Walked with Adam and Eve in the Garden
Which verse talks about the joy of living in God's presence?

Describe what you think it might have been like for Adam and Eve to live in the garden with God.

The Ology of Sin

12. Sin
How does Mark 12:30 tell us that we are supposed to love God?

What was Satan's first sin? Hint: See Isaiah 14:13–14.

13. Satan's First Temptation
How does the Bible tell us to fight the devil?

How does Jesus tell us to fight the devil?

14. Sin Entered the World Through Adam
When does David say our sinfulness begins?

What percentage of people who have lived on the earth have sinned?

15. Sin Separates Us from God and from Each Other
How does sin affect your relationship with God?

16. Sin Always Brings Judgment
Besides Eve, whom else does the Bible tell us the serpent will try to deceive?

What passage describes the curse upon Adam?

17. God's Promise of Salvation
Who is the one man through whom sin came? Who is the one man who will reverse the curse of sin?

What did God do to provide clothing for Adam and Eve and how does that point to Jesus?

18. God Sent Adam and Eve out of the Garden
Why did God block the way to the tree of life?

In what verse do we see the tree of life restored?

19. Sin Spreads like a Disease
What did God decide to do about the sin on the earth at the time of Noah?

Did the flood wipe out the sin in the hearts of men and women?

The Ology of the Promise and the Law

20. God Makes a Promise
Did Abraham know where God was sending him?

Read Hebrews 11:1 and write a definition of faith using your own words.

21. God Keeps His Promise
Which verse talks about God keeping his promise (his covenant)?

Even though God delivered his people from slavery, how do we know they still had trouble trusting him?

22. The Ten Commandments of God
What is the first of the Ten Commandments?

What is the new commandment Jesus gave us in the New Testament?

Rewrite Luke 10:27 in your own words.

23. Breaking One Law Breaks the Whole Law
What do we become conscious, or aware of, through the law?

When Jesus tells us to "be perfect" (Matthew 5:48), what kind of perfection is he talking about? Hint: Look back at Matthew 5:44.

24. God's Holiness Cannot Be in the Same Place as Sin
Which verse tells us that if we were to see the face of God in our sinful state we would die?

What is our only hope when we one day face God's judgment?

25. God Gave a Way to Cover Sin
Which verses use the word *atonement*?

What part of the animal does the Bible tell us makes atonement for our life?

26. Jesus Is the Sacrifice We Need
What two Scripture passages say that God will take away our sin?

The Ology of Christ

27. The Son of God Comes to Earth
How is Jesus described in 1 Timothy 6:15–16?

Which of the five senses does John mention in 1 John 1:1? Why does what he writes make his gospel more believable?

28. The Son Stepped off His Throne
List all the verses in this section that refer to Jesus's work as Savior.

What did Jesus have to do to accomplish his saving work?

29. Jesus Always Loved God and People
How are you as a child growing up different from Jesus?

Which verse tells us how we can fight the devil's temptations?

30. Jesus Is Completely Human
Why was it important for Jesus to be fully man?

Which verse tells us what we must do to have our sins wiped out?

31. Jesus Is Completely God
Which Scripture passage in this section does the best job showing that Jesus was God? Give a reason to support your answer.

Why did the people want to stone Jesus?

32. Jesus Died in Our Place

Which verse tells us that Jesus became sin for us?

What Scripture passage foretold that Jesus would die for his people long before it ever happened?

33. Jesus's Resurrection Defeated Death

Pick three Scripture passages that show the Trinity at work in raising Jesus from the dead. Find verses for Jesus, God the Father, and the Holy Spirit.

What was the hope expressed by David in Psalm 16 and quoted in Acts 2:24–28?

34. We Are Safely Hidden in Christ

What are four things the verses say we have by being "in Christ"?

Which of the verses in this section is your favorite? Give a reason why.

35. Jesus Sends His Disciples on a Mission

In which verse did Jesus send his disciples out to call more disciples and baptize them?

What did Jesus show his disciples when he appeared to them after the resurrection?

The Ology of the Holy Spirit

36. Jesus Promised to Send the Holy Spirit

Of what did Jesus say the Holy Spirit would remind them?

Why can't the world accept the truth about the Holy Spirit?

37. The Spirit Arrives on Pentecost

Which of the verses contain a prophecy by the prophet Joel predicting the outpouring of God's Spirit?

What two things happened to the people filled with the Holy Spirit at Pentecost?

38. The Holy Spirit: God's Best Gift

What will the Holy Spirit guide us into?

Who did the prophet Joel say God was going to pour his Spirit on in the last days?

The Ology of Adoption into God's Family

39. Chosen

What different words does the Bible use to describe the fact that God knew us and selected us for salvation before we were born? ("predestined" [Ephesians 1:5]; "chosen" [1 Peter 2:9]; "foreknew" [Romans 8:29])

What two verses tell us that people are dead in their sins before God saves them?

40. Called

What did God use to call us?

Which verse says that the "God of all grace . . . has called us to his eternal glory in Christ"?

41. Born Again

What verse tells us that we become a new creation in Christ when we are born again?

What kind of heart will God take away from his children and what kind of heart will he replace it with?

42. Faith

How do we know we are truly children of God?

What three things did Paul tell King Agrippa he did to make sure he was faithful to the message he was given?

43. Jesus Paid It All

Which verse tells us that we are "not justified by works of the law but through faith in Jesus Christ"?

What two things do Romans 10:9 tell us we need to do in order to be saved?

44. Adopted

To whom did God give the right to become children of God?

Which verse explains that God disciplines all those he accepts as his children for their good?

The Ology of Change

45. Sin Isn't in Charge Anymore

What two kinds of slavery are mentioned in the verses in this section? Give verse references.

46. Set Apart, Holy for God

What did Paul tell the Ephesians they were chosen for?

Which four Scripture passages use a form of the word *sanctified*?

47. We Grow a Little at a Time

Which Scripture gives us a picture of how Jesus is changing us by washing us with water through the word?

Which verses describes our growing to be more like Jesus by saying that we are being transformed into his "image from one degree of glory to another"?

48. Put off the Old, Put on the New

Name a few sins that you often struggle with.

How do we combat sin in our lives—the old ways of living?

49. The Holy Spirit Helps Us Fight Against Sin

Which image is used to describe our struggle against sin in Romans 7:21–23?

List some ways that the Holy Spirit helps us to fight against sin.

50. The Fruit of the Spirit

What is the difference between the acts of the flesh and the fruit of the Spirit?

51. Running the Race to the End

Which of the verses tells us that Jesus won't lose any of his children running the race by saying "no one will snatch them out of my hand"?

Which verse mentions a prize? What or who is the prize?

The Ology of the Church

52. The Church Is Built with Living Stones

What is the spiritual house being referred to in 1 Peter 2:5–6?

Which of the verses describes the church as a "dwelling place for God"?

53. The Church Is God's Temple

What is Paul trying to teach us when he says that Christians working together are like a body (1 Corinthians 12:14–18)?

Who is the head of the body described in the Scripture passages in this section?

54. We Gather to Worship
What are the two things Jesus said must be a part of our worship?

What reason does the writer of the book of Hebrews give us for worshiping God in reverence and awe?

55. The Lord's Supper
Why did Jesus tell us to copy what he did in the Last Supper?

Which passage tells us not to drink the cup of the Lord in an "unworthy manner"? What does it mean to drink the cup in this way?

56. Baptism
Which verse mentions the Trinity—the Father, Son, and Holy Spirit?

What did Peter command the crowd to do in Acts 2:38?

57. The Gifts of the Spirit
List the spiritual gifts listed in the verses. Name two people you know who have one of these gifts.

What does 1 Corinthians 13:8 say about spiritual gifts? What will never end?

58. Persecution of the Saints
What did Jesus say about those who are persecuted in Matthew 5:11?

Which two Scripture passages talk about Christians being scattered because of persecution?

The Ology of the End Times

59. A Picture of the Future
In which verse does God declare that he announces things in his Word that have not yet taken place to show his glory?

What clues about the future do the verses in this section give us?

60. The Return of Christ
How does Luke say the Son of Man—Jesus—will come when he returns?

The Bible tells us that we should encourage one another with the details of Jesus's return and the resurrection of our bodies. Read through the Scripture passages and write down at least one thing you are excited or encouraged about from each passage.

61. The Final Judgment
At the final judgment, what will unbelievers have to give account for?

Who will be afraid when Jesus returns?

62. A Very Different Day for All God's Children
Which passage speaks of God's amazing forgiveness for those who trust in him?

How can you lay up treasure in heaven (Matthew 6:19–20)?

63. The New Heavens and Earth
How will the new heavens and earth be like the Garden of Eden before Adam and Eve sinned?

Which of the Scripture verses most makes you want Jesus to return and make the earth new again?

64. The Special Place Where God Lives with His People

What will be the light of the re-created earth (see Revelation 21:17–27)?

In your own words, what does Jesus tell his disciples about heaven in John 14:2–3?

65. The Final Wedding

How many times did John the Baptist call Jesus the Bridegroom in John 3:25–30?

In Ephesians 5:22–31 Jesus is pictured as a husband. Who is his bride in that passage?

The Ology of God's Word

66. God Wrote the Bible Through People

Who did Peter say carried the prophets along and enabled them to speak for God?

In 1 Corinthians 2:12–13, Paul writes that his words did not come from human wisdom. Where did he say they came from?

67. God's Word Is True

How can Hebrews 6:18 encourage us to trust the Bible?

What do we learn about God's Word in Numbers 23:19?

68. God Talks to You and You Talk to God

Divide the Lord's Prayer (Matthew 6:9–13) into its two major parts and write a title for each. (The first part of the Lord's Prayer (Matthew 6:9–10) is about giving God the glory due his name. The second part requests help from God for daily living.)

Rewrite Philippians 4:6 in your own words. Then write out a prayer to God.

69. The Bible Is Our Spiritual Food

What did Jeremiah do with God's words?

What do you think it means to eat God's words?

70. The Holy Spirit Helps Us Understand God's Word

Which verse describes those with hardened hearts being alienated or separated from God?

What do those who live according to the Spirit set their minds on?

71. The Word of God Lives Forever

How long did Jesus say his Word would last?

What do all the Bible passages in this section have in common?

Think Theology, Talk Theology

1. God Always Was and Always Will Be

List all the names and characteristics for God mentioned in the Scripture verses in this chapter. (God endures forever; God is eternal, everlasting; God lives forever and ever; God's years have no end; he is Wonderful Counselor, Mighty God, Everlasting Father, Prince of Peace, Bread of Life, Deliverer, Hope of Israel, the Good Shepherd, King of Ages.)

2. God Is Three in One

Which of the verses mentions all three persons of the Trinity together in one place? (In Matthew 3:16–17 when Jesus is baptized, onlookers hear the Father's voice, and see the Spirit descend in the form of a dove.)

Read John 14:26. How does it explain the Trinity? (This verse explains how the Father gives us the Holy Spirit in the name of Jesus. It is the Holy Spirit who teaches us and helps us to recall what Jesus said.)

3. God Created Everything out of Nothing at All

Who does Colossians 1:16 refer to? (Jesus, the Son of God, and his work in creation.)

What does the passage from Isaiah tell us we can learn about God from his work in creation? (The created world carries the imprint of God's glory.)

4. God Is All-Powerful

What proclaims God's handiwork? (The heavens and the sky above [Psalm 19:1])

What verse tells us that people have no excuse for refusing to believe in God? (Romans 1:20)

5. God Is in Control

What does God command to fall upon the earth? (Snow and rain [Job 37:5–6])

What does every man and woman get from God? (God gives life and breath and everything [Acts 17:25].)

6. God Knows All Things

Which verse tells us that God knows everything? (1 John 3:20)

Rewrite Hebrews 4:13 in your own words. Describe how this verse makes you feel. (Many possible answers.)

7. God Is Everywhere
Rewrite Psalm 139:7–10 in your own words. (Many possible answers.)

8. God Is Perfect
Which verse(s) tells us what perfect love looks like? (1 Corinthians 13:4–7)

Who do you find hard to love? What can you do to love them better? (Many possible answers.)

9. God Created Man and Woman in His Image
In whose likeness did God create man and woman? Which verse tells us that? (In God's likeness. Genesis 5:1–2)

List some ways that men and women are different from animals? (We can understand God's Word, sing, love, speak, and worship God.)

10. The First Husband and Wife
How are men and women the same? How are they different? (They are both created in the image of God. God gave them different jobs and roles.)

What did Adam name the wife God created from his rib? (Adam named her Woman because she was taken out of man [Genesis 2:22–23].)

11. God Walked with Adam and Eve in the Garden
Which verse talks about the joy of living in God's presence? (Psalm 16:11)

Describe what you think it might have been like for Adam and Eve to live in the garden with God. (Many possible answers.)

12. Sin
How does Mark 12:30 tell us that we are supposed to love God? (We are to love God with all our heart, soul, mind, and strength.)

What was Satan's first sin? Hint: See Isaiah 14:13–14. (Satan wanted to BE God.)

13. Satan's First Temptation
How does the Bible tell us to fight the devil? (Hold to a "sincere and pure devotion to Christ" [2 Corinthians 11:3]; submit to God and resist the devil [James 4:7]; watch and pray [Matthew 26:41].)

How does Jesus tell us to fight the devil? (He taught us to pray, "Lead us not into temptation" [Matthew 6:13].)

14. Sin Entered the World Through Adam
When does David say our sinfulness begins? (We are sinners from the time we are conceived [Psalm 51:5].)

What percentage of people who have lived on the earth have sinned? (One hundred percent—all have sinned [Romans 3:23; Ecclesiastes 7:20].)

15. Sin Separates Us from God and from Each Other
How does sin affect your relationship with God? (Sin makes it hard to pray and separates us from God [Ezra 9:6; Ephesians 2:12].)

16. Sin Always Brings Judgment
Besides Eve, who else does the Bible tell us the serpent will try to deceive? (The serpent will try to deceive any believer he can [2 Corinthians 11:3].)

What passage describes the curse upon Adam? (Genesis 3:17-18)

17. God's Promise of Salvation

Who is the one man through whom sin came? Who is the one man who will reverse the curse of sin? (Adam, Jesus Christ [see Romans 5:17])

What did God do to provide clothing for Adam and Eve and how does that point to Jesus? (He killed animals to provide skins to cover them [Genesis 3:21]. The death of those animals point to Jesus dying on the cross for our sin.)

18. God Sent Adam and Eve out of the Garden

Why did God block the way to the tree of life? (If Adam and Eve ate from the tree of life they would live forever. Because of their sin they could not escape death [Genesis 3:22–24].)

In what verse do we see the tree of life restored? (Revelation 22:2)

19. Sin Spreads like a Disease

What did God decide to do about the sin on the earth at the time of Noah? (God decided to wipe out the people he had made [Genesis 6:7, 13].)

Did the flood wipe out the sin in the hearts of men and women? (No, see Genesis 8:21.)

20. God Makes a Promise

Did Abraham know where God was sending him? (No, see Hebrews 11:8.)

Read Hebrews 11:1 and write a definition of faith using your own words. (Many possible answers.)

21. God Keeps His Promise

Which verse talks about God keeping his promise (his covenant)? (Exodus 2:24 talks about God keeping his promise to Israel.)

Even though God delivered his people from slavery, how do we know they still had trouble trusting him? (Exodus 17:3 says that God's people complained that they didn't have any water to drink; they didn't trust God.)

22. The Ten Commandments of God

What is the first of the Ten Commandments? ("I am the Lord your God, who brought you out of Egypt, out of the land of slavery. You shall have no other gods before me" [Exodus 20:2–3].)

What is the new commandment Jesus gave us in the New Testament? (To love one another as Jesus has loved us [John 13:34].)

Rewrite Luke 10:27 in your own words. (Many possible answers.)

23. Breaking One Law Breaks the Whole Law

What do we become conscious, or aware of, through the law? (Sin [Romans 3:20].)

When Jesus tells us to "be perfect" (Matthew 5:48), what kind of perfection is he talking about? Hint: Look back at Matthew 5:44. (Jesus is talking here about loving perfectly—about loving others like God has loved us.)

24. God's Holiness Cannot Be in the Same Place as Sin

Which verse tells us that if we were to see the face of God in our sinful state we would die? (Exodus 33:20)

What is our only hope when we one day face God's judgment? (Jesus, the spotless Lamb of God died for our sins [John 1:29].)

25. God Gave a Way to Cover Sin
Which verses use the word *atonement*? (Leviticus 1:4; 4:35; 17:11)

What part of the animal does the Bible tell us makes atonement for our life? (The shed blood, see Leviticus 17:11.)

26. Jesus Is the Sacrifice We Need
What two Scripture passages say that God will take away our sin? (Isaiah 53:5–6; Psalm 103:11–12)

27. The Son of God Comes to Earth
How is Jesus described in 1 Timothy 6:15–16? (He is the blessed and only Sovereign, the King of kings and Lord of lords, who is immortal and who lives in "unapproachable light.")

Which of the five senses does John mention in 1 John 1:1? Why does what he writes make his gospel more believable? (John mentions sight, hearing, and touch. These make his testimony about Jesus believable because he is an eyewitness to what he is writing about.)

28. The Son Stepped off His Throne
List all the verses in this section that refer to Jesus's work as Savior. (Isaiah 33:22; 49:6; Matthew 1:21; Luke 1:69, 71, 77)

What did Jesus have to do to accomplish his saving work? (Jesus had to live the perfect life that we could never live. He then died on the cross taking the punishment that we deserved for our sins on himself. When we trust in Jesus, God says that we are righteous.)

29. Jesus Always Loved God and People
How are you as a child growing up different from Jesus? (We are all sinners. Unlike Jesus, who was sinless, we sin every day.)

Which verse tells us how we can fight the devil's temptations? (James 4:7)

30. Jesus Is Completely Human
Why was it important for Jesus to be fully man? (Jesus had to be fully and completely a man to die in our place because the punishment God was storing up was for man.)

Which verse tells us what we must do to have our sins wiped out? (Acts 3:19)

31. Jesus Is Completely God
Which Scripture passage in this section does the best job showing that Jesus was God? Give a reason to support your answer. (Many possible answers.)

Why did the people want to stone Jesus? (They wanted to stone Jesus because they thought he was sinning—committing blasphemy—by claiming to be God [John 10:33].)

32. Jesus Died in Our Place
Which verse tells us that Jesus became sin for us? (2 Corinthians 5:21)

What Scripture passage foretold that Jesus would die for his people long before it ever happened? (Isaiah 53:5–6)

33. Jesus's Resurrection Defeated Death

Pick three Scripture passages that show the Trinity at work in raising Jesus from the dead. Find verses for Jesus, God the Father, and the Holy Spirit. (Jesus—John 10:18; God the Father—1 Corinthians 6:14 and Acts 2:24; the Holy Spirit—Romans 8:11)

What was the hope expressed by David in Psalm 16 and quoted in Acts 2:24–28? (David expressed the certainty that even after death he would live in God's presence.)

34. We Are Safely Hidden in Christ

What are four things the verses say we have by being "in Christ"? (Eternal life [Romans 6:23]; no condemnation [Romans 8:1]; freedom from the law [Romans 8:2]; the love of God [Romans 8:39])

Which of the verses in this section is your favorite? Give a reason why. (Many possible answers.)

35. Jesus Sends His Disciples on a Mission

In which verse did Jesus send his disciples out to call more disciples and baptize them? (Matthew 28:19)

What did Jesus show his disciples when he appeared to them after the resurrection? (He showed them his hands and feet so they could see the wound marks and believe that it really was him [Luke 24:39].)

36. Jesus Promised to Send the Holy Spirit

Of what did Jesus say the Holy Spirit would remind them? (The Holy Spirit would remind them of everything Jesus had said to them [John 14:26].)

Why can't the world accept the truth about the Holy Spirit? (The world neither sees the Holy Spirit nor knows him [John 14:17].)

37. The Spirit Arrives on Pentecost

Which of the verses contain a prophecy by the prophet Joel predicting the outpouring of God's Spirit? (Acts 2:14–17)

What two things happened to the people filled with the Holy Spirit at Pentecost? (They had tongues of fire appear over their heads and they spoke in other tongues [Acts 2:3–4].)

38. The Holy Spirit: God's Best Gift

What will the Holy Spirit guide us into? (The Holy Spirit will guide us into all truth [John 16:13].)

Who did the prophet Joel say God was going to pour his Spirit on in the last days? (The prophet Joel said God would pour out his Spirit on all people in the last days [Acts 2:16–18].)

39. Chosen

What different words does the Bible use to describe the fact that God knew us and selected us for salvation before we were born? ("predestined" [Ephesians 1:5]; "chosen" [1 Peter 2:9]; "foreknew" [Romans 8:29])

What two verses tell us that people are dead in their sins before God saves them? (Ephesians 2:1–3; Colossians 2:13)

40. Called

What did God use to call us? (God used the gospel to call us out of darkness into light, [2 Thessalonians 2:14].)

Which verse says that the "God of all grace . . . has called us to his eternal glory in Christ"? (1 Peter 5:10)

41. Born Again
What verse tells us that we become a new creation in Christ when we are born again? (2 Corinthians 5:17)

What kind of heart will God take away from his children and what kind of heart will he replace it with? (God will take away a heart of stone and give us a heart of flesh [Ezekiel 36:26].)

42. Faith
How do we know we are truly children of God? (We know we are children of God if we love him and carry out his commands [1 John 3:9–10].)

What three things did Paul tell King Agrippa he did to make sure he was faithful to the message he was given? (Paul preached that people should repent, turn their hearts to God, and demonstrate their repentance by their deeds [Acts 26:20].)

43. Jesus Paid It All
Which verse tells us that we are "not justified by works of the law but through faith in Jesus Christ"? (Galatians 2:16)

What two things do Romans 10:9 tell us we need to do in order to be saved? (Confess with our mouth that Jesus Christ is Lord, and believe in our heart that God raised him up from the dead.)

44. Adopted
To whom did God give the right to become children of God? (God gave the right to become children of God to all who did receive him, to those who believed in his name [John 1:12].)

Which verse explains that God disciplines all those he accepts as his children for their good? (Hebrews 12:7)

45. Sin Isn't in Charge Anymore
What two kinds of slavery are mentioned in the verses in this section? Give verse references. (Slavery to sin—Romans 6:6–7, 17; and slavery to righteousness—Romans 6:18–19)

46. Set Apart, Holy for God
What did Paul tell the Ephesians they were chosen for? (They were chosen before the creation of the world to be holy and blameless in his sight [Ephesians 1:4].)

Which four Scripture passages use a form of the word *sanctified*? (2 Thessalonians 2:13; 1 Peter 1:1–2; Acts 20:32; 1 Corinthians 6:11)

47. We Grow a Little at a Time
Which Scripture gives us a picture of how Jesus is changing us by washing us with water through the word? (Ephesians 5:25–27)

Which verses describes our growing to be more like Jesus by saying that we are being transformed into his "image from one degree of glory to another"? (2 Corinthians 3:18)

48. Put off the Old, Put on the New
Name a few sins that you often struggle with. (Many possible answers.)

How do we combat sin in our lives—the old ways of living? (walk by the Spirit [Galatians 5:16])

49. The Holy Spirit Helps Us Fight Against Sin
Which image is used to describe our struggle against sin in Romans 7:21–23? (Sin is described as a war.)

List some ways that the Holy Spirit helps us to fight against sin. (The Holy Spirit will teach and remind us of what Jesus said [John 14:26]; the Holy Spirit will lead us into all truth [John 16:13]; the Holy Spirit helps us pray [Romans 8:26].)

50. The Fruit of the Spirit
What is the difference between the acts of the flesh and the fruit of the Spirit? (The acts of the flesh, whether they look good or bad, are the result of living life apart from the Holy Spirit; the fruit of the Spirit is what the Holy Spirit alone produces in our lives.)

51. Running the Race to the End
Which of the verses tells us that Jesus won't lose any of his children running the race by saying "no one will snatch them out of my hand"? (John 10:28)

Which verse mentions a prize? What or who is the prize? (First Corinthians 9:24 tells us to run in such a way to get the prize. The prize is living forever with Jesus in heaven.)

52. The Church Is Built with Living Stones
What is the spiritual house being referred to in 1 Peter 2:5–6? (The spiritual house is the church.)

Which of the verses describes the church as a "dwelling place for God"? (Ephesians 2:22)

53. The Church Is God's Temple
What is Paul trying to teach us when he says that Christians working together are like a body (1 Corinthians 12:14–18)? (We need each other and the different gifts we each have. Every believer has a part to play in God's church.)

Who is the head of the body described in the Scripture passages in this section? (Jesus Christ is the head of the body [Colossians 1:18].)

54. We Gather to Worship
What are the two things Jesus said must be a part of our worship? ("Those who worship [God] must worship in spirit and truth" [John 4:24]. This means that our words should contain truth and we should obey God's truth and follow the leading of the Spirit in everything we do.)

What reason does the writer of the book of Hebrews give us for worshiping God in reverence and awe? (We should worship God in reverence and awe because of the amazing kingdom, which cannot be shaken, that he has given us. [Hebrews 12:28])

55. The Lord's Supper
Why did Jesus tell us to copy what he did in the Last Supper? (Jesus said we should do these things to remember what he did for us [Luke 22:19].)

Which passage tells us not to drink the cup of the Lord in an "unworthy manner"? What does it mean to drink the cup in this way? (First Corinthians 11:27 talks about drinking the cup of the Lord in an "unworthy manner," which means doing it without confessing our sins and keeping our sins hidden.)

56. Baptism
Which verse mentions the Trinity—the Father, Son, and Holy Spirit? (Matthew 28:19)

What did Peter command the crowd to do in Acts 2:38? (Peter commanded them to repent and be baptized.)

57. The Gifts of the Spirit
List the spiritual gifts listed in the verses. Name two people you know who have one of these gifts. (Many possible answers.)

What does 1 Corinthians 13:8 say about spiritual gifts? What will never end? (While prophecies and other gifts will cease, love will always remain.)

58. Persecution of the Saints
What did Jesus say about those who are persecuted in Matthew 5:11? (Jesus said that those who are persecuted are blessed.)

Which two Scripture passages talk about Christians being scattered because of persecution? (Acts 8:1–4; 11:19)

59. A Picture of the Future
In which verse does God declare that he announces things in his Word that have not yet taken place to show his glory? (Isaiah 42:9).

What clues about the future do the verses in this section give us? (Jesus is coming soon [Revelation 22:7]; there will be difficult times in the last days [2 Timothy 3:1]; scoffers will come in the last days [2 Peter 3:3]; one day the Lord will be king over the whole earth [Zechariah 14:9].)

60. The Return of Christ
How does Luke say the Son of Man—Jesus—will come when he returns? (The Son of Man will come "in a cloud with power and great glory" [Luke 21:27].)

The Bible tells us that we should encourage one another with the details of Jesus's return and the resurrection of our bodies. Read through the Scrip-

ture passages and write down at least one thing you are excited or encouraged about from each passage. (Many possible answers.)

61. The Final Judgment
At the final judgment, what will unbelievers have to give account for? (Every careless word they speak [Matthew 12:36].)

Who will be afraid when Jesus returns? (All those will be afraid who don't fear the name of the Lord now—those who do not trust Jesus for salvation [Malachi 4:1–3].)

62. A Very Different Day for All God's Children
Which passage speaks of God's amazing forgiveness for those who trust in him? (Psalm 103:10–12).

How can you lay up treasure in heaven (Matthew 6:19–20)? (Serve Jesus here on earth by loving others and telling them about him.)

63. The New Heavens and Earth
How will the new heavens and earth be like the Garden of Eden before Adam and Eve sinned? (There will be no sickness or death. We will have the tree of life and a river of life, but the most amazing thing will be that God himself will be with us.)

Which of the Scripture verses most makes you want Jesus to return and make the earth new again? (Several possible answers.)

64. The Special Place Where God Lives with His People
What will be the light of the re-created earth (see Revelation 21:17–27)? (Revelation 21:23 tells us the glory of God will light up the city and the lamp will be the Lamb.)

In your own words, what does Jesus tell his disciples about heaven in John 14:2–3? (God's house has many rooms; Jesus is going to prepare a place for his people and then he will come and get them and take them to live with him forever.)

65. The Final Wedding
How many times did John the Baptist call Jesus the Bridegroom in John 3:25–30? (John called Jesus the Bridegroom three times.)

In Ephesians 5:22–31 Jesus is pictured as a husband. Who is his bride in that passage?
(The bride is the church.)

66. God Wrote the Bible Through People
Who did Peter say carried the prophets along and enabled them to speak for God? (The Holy Spirit carried the prophets along.)

In 1 Corinthians 2:12–13, Paul writes that his words did not come from human wisdom. Where did he say they came from? (They were taught by the Holy Spirit.)

67. God's Word Is True
How can Hebrews 6:18 encourage us to trust the Bible? (Since God cannot lie, and the Bible is his Word, we know we can trust that what it says is true.)

What do we learn about God's Word in Numbers 23:19? (We learn that God is not like man who lies. Everything God says he will do; everything he promises he will fulfill.)

68. God Talks to You and You Talk to God
Divide the Lord's Prayer (Matthew 6:9–13) into its two major parts and write a title for each. (The first part of the Lord's Prayer (Matthew 6:9–10) is about giving God the glory due his name. The second part requests help from God for daily living.)

Rewrite Philippians 4:6 in your own words. Then write out a prayer to God. (Many possible answers.)

69. The Bible Is Our Spiritual Food
What did Jeremiah do with God's words? (Jeremiah ate God's words [Jeremiah 15:16].)

What do you think it means to eat God's words? (To eat God's words is an expression that means that Jeremiah took God's words into his mind and heart and obeyed them so that he benefitted from them.)

70. The Holy Spirit Helps Us Understand God's Word
Which verse describes those with hardened hearts being alienated or separated from God? (Ephesians 4:18)

What do those who live according to the Spirit set their minds on? (Those who live according to the Spirit "set their minds on the things of the Spirit" [Romans 8:5].)

71. The Word of God Lives Forever
How long did Jesus say his Word would last? (Jesus said that heaven and earth would pass away but his Word would not pass away [Matthew 24:35].)

What do all the Bible passages in this section have in common? (They all talk about how God's Word will stand forever, be fixed in the heavens forever, and never pass away.)

Be sure to check out the musical companion to *The Ology*!

Find sheet music, resources, and more info at www.SovereignGraceMusic.org